UNDOING THE KNOTS

Reclaiming Our Good

CYNTHIA PAULSEN

Contents

For those who believe in the Good.
I see you, I hear you,
and I support your intentions with Love.

Introduction

What are *knots*, and why do they need to be undone? For the purpose of this book, knots are the perceived problems, challenges, and negative experiences of life that we all encounter. Knots can appear as sickness, disease, lack, loss, loneliness, fear, frustration, problems, accidents, obstacles, conflict, discomfort, suffering, etc. Admittedly, knots can be messy, frustrating, and painful at times, but our knots are not the focus of this book.

The focus of this book is the *undoing*. As spiritual seekers, we know it is never about the problems we encounter; it is about how we spiritually handle and respond to our knots. We want them undone quickly and easily because we all want (and more importantly, we all deserve) to live in peace and harmony. This is not a "How-To" book, but rather, a "How-About-This?" book. Based on my work as an independent New Thought Minister and Spiritual Practitioner, it is a collection of practices, rituals, and illustrations designed to navigate life's difficulties and support the undoing of knots.

Every minister I have ever met studies, practices, and writes. I am no exception. This book was born from the many years I have spent studying transformative spirituality, applying spiritual practices, and writing blogs, sermons, keynote addresses, and workshops. The stories, lessons, and meditations come from my own personal, winding path toward God, as an interfaith, inter-spiritual seeker and teacher.

I believe that everything we could possibly want or need is within us. We can experience health, harmony, love, joy, peace, abundance — any good thing we desire. How? By applying universal spiritual principles and using the spiritual practices that are available to us. There is no limit to the good we can experience! It is my life passion and divine purpose to share these ideas with you.

What follows is a compilation of essays about various ways to undo our knots and reclaim our good. For easy reference, the spiritual practice or principle with which the essay is concerned is underneath the essay title. They contain bits from New Thought philosophies with a sprinkling of various other faith traditions. Drawing from my experience with the United Church of Christ, Disciples of Christ, the American Interfaith Holistic Temple, Unity Church, Centers for Spiritual Living, Spiritualism, and Divine Science Church, they cover a wide range of topics. They explore the power of our word and the significance of our thoughts; seasonal holidays and liturgical occasions; current event themes such as politics and disasters; sacred rituals; spiritual practice; and always with the oneness, oneness, oneness. These essays are about learning new ways to reveal our good, and truly, my friends, they are my prayer for us all.

May our knots be undone.
May our obstacles be cleared. May our fears be calmed.
May we know the truth of our unity with Spirit.
May what remains... be extraordinarily good.

Undoing the Knots

INTERFAITH/HONORING ALL PATHS TO GOD

During the turbulent, locked-down months of 2020, I attended a weekly spiritual empowerment session via Zoom with my Center for Spiritual Living (CSL) senior minister and many others. Participants shared how they were coping (with their knots) and made prayer requests. That is where I got to know Shirley, a charming older woman originally from Guatemala who had practiced Catholicism for most of her life. Shirley is upbeat and positive, spiritually aware, and quite devout in her adoration of God. 2020 was rough on Shirley, as it was for most of us. Amidst the Covid-19 pandemic, the often violent protests against police brutality and racism, the contentious election, economic concerns, and supply chain shortages, etc., Shirley admitted that she had gone back to praying The Holy Rosary regularly, turning to various saints for comfort, guidance, and protection. When faced with an inordinate number of challenging, stressful life conditions, her inclination was to revert back to the spiritual rituals she found most comforting and natural.

Shirley told us she had been praying to Our Lady, Undoer of Knots, for obstacles to be cleared, kinks to be released, and problems to be unraveled and resolved not only in her own life, but in the whole world. This idea intrigued me. The visual of our problems, no matter how big or small, existing only as knots to ultimately be undone, resonated. Isn't that what we do? We get ourselves tied up in knots, whether real or imagined. We create our own obstacles, obstructions, kinks, and troubles with our false thoughts and beliefs.

After reading more about Our Lady, Undoer of Knots, I learned that the devotion is directed to Mary, mother of Jesus, and the idea— the spiritual principle, really — is that Mary represents a loving mother who never refuses to come to the aid of a child, any child. Thinking back to my own childhood, any time I played with a necklace chain, a rope, or string and found it stuck in knots — try as I might, I couldn't unravel it — but when I took it to my mother, she inevitably worked her magic.

Mothers are good at unraveling our knots. The famous Baroque painting by Johann Georg Schmidtner, "Mary, Undoer of Knots," depicts the Blessed Virgin Mary surrounded by angels, as she unties knots from a ribbon. Catholics pray to her, asking her to take their knots into her hands and undo them for the glory of God. The prayer concludes with a heartfelt request for guidance, protection, and refuge.

Our Lady, Undoer of Knots, bears spiritual resemblance to the elephant-headed Hindu Deity Ganesha, also known as the Lord of Obstacles, popularly worshipped for his wisdom as a remover of obstacles. People pray to him before starting something new, to make their way straight and clear, free from troubles. The Sanskrit mantra associated with him is *Om Gam Ganapataye Namaha*, which translates to: "Salutations to the remover of obstacles" or "I bow to you, Lord Ganesha." Repeating this mantra aloud, over and over, can be very grounding. It clears the mind, offering an opportunity to be present in the moment.

The Ganesha mantra practice is not unlike the Buddhist practice of chanting the beloved mantra *Om Mani Padme Hum*, which translates to "Hail to the Jewel in the Lotus." Many believe that this particular chant calms fears, soothes concerns, invokes the qualities of compassion, and achieves peace. These Hindu and Buddhist rituals are akin to the Catholic devotion to Our Lady, Undoer of Knots — all methods to shift focus to the powerful truth that all is well, all obstacles are made clear, all knots ultimately come undone. These three examples are different spiritual practices from different faith traditions. The underlying powerful spiritual truth is the same:

Clarity comes. Prayer is answered.
Goodness — the good that is rightfully ours —
is reclaimed and ultimately revealed.

These practices are not much different than doing a spiritual mind treatment or affirmative prayer, a practice rooted in New Thought Principle. Praying affirmatively intends to shift our mind so we can manifest what we desire, recognizing the infinite Spirit of God and our unification with that very presence of God. It is from this place — the place of our unity with God — that we remember and realize that all is well. For many spiritual seekers, this is where (and how) the knots come undone and our good is reclaimed and revealed to us.

Ernest Holmes, founder of the Religious Science movement and what later became the CSL organization, explained the power of this unification with this Spirit of God in his What We Believe statement, also known as the Declaration of Principles:

We believe in God, the living Spirit Almighty; one, indestructible, absolute, and self-existent Cause. This One manifests Itself in and through all creation, but is not absorbed by Its creation. The manifest universe is the body of God; it is the logical and necessary outcome of the infinite self-knowingness of God. We believe in the individualization of the Spirit in us, and that all people are individualizations of the One Spirit.[1]

Our unity with Source is of natural consequence, for each of us is, individually, a child of God. As the Bible teaches, "That which is born of Spirit is spirit" (John 3:6). Our natural state is divine; each of us is a unique expression of Spirit. This means that I am an expression of Spirit. You are an expression of Spirit. Everyone and everything is an expression of Spirit. Praying to the Blessed Virgin Mary, repeating a mantra to Ganesha, chanting a Buddhist mantra, writing a spiritual mind treatment, exploring our own inner consciousness for help with our perceived troubles and obstacles — all of these methods are like asking Spirit Itself, the Spirit within us, for help.

These spiritual practices (and of course there are many others) are pathways to the "heaven within" each of us. The rituals, from whatever spiritual path, are all useful in their own right. The rituals, dare I say, don't matter as much as the motivation behind them. The effectiveness of a spiritual practice does not depend upon the form followed, but upon the spirit involved. Whatever method, practice, or ritual that frees us from heaviness and lifts our spirits is what we should do. Spiritual practice is an attitude, a conscious decision, and ultimately, an elegant turning of one's soul toward the One Universal Presence and Spirit of God. Thankfully, the One Spirit of God is what is real and true.

The rope or ribbon in the Our Lady, Undoer of Knots prayer symbolizes our unity with the Spirit of God, and assuredly, it is real. The knots, however, are not real. Our task is to remember that the problems, unwanted conditions, and undesirable experiences we may go through in our lives are not real. What is real is our unity with the One. It is smooth, straight, and stable. It is changeless, constant, and eternal. The knots are self-manufactured, false, removable, and always changeable. The rituals and methods we use to undo our knots are as varied as the knots themselves, but they lead us to the same realization. They reveal the goodness of God, the good God intends for our lives.

Perhaps you find yourself struggling with your knots from time to time, as Shirley does, and as I do. As spiritual beings, we can logically and intellectually know that the power of God lies within us, yet simultaneously be exhausted by current events and our present life experience. On the one hand, we can trust in our unity with the One Spirit, and on the other hand, have very human-like doubts about our ability to manage and persevere. This is a reminder to give yourself some grace.

The spiritual truth is that the more we focus on the living Spirit of God, the more our good is revealed to us. As the knots come undone, the easier it is to claim our good. What is our good? Any good thing we may desire. Loving relationships, financial abundance, a body free from illness and disease, fulfillment and life purpose, health, harmony, peace, joy, and the list goes on and on.

There is no limit to our good, for with God, there is no limit.

As We Believe

OBSERVING THOUGHTS AND BELIEFS

Matt. 8:13 "... as you have believed,
let it be done for you."
Matt. 9:22 "... your faith has made you well."
Matt. 9:29 "... according to your faith,
let it be done to you."

Who doesn't love a good "Jesus performs a miracle" story? We all do, and fortunately, the Bible is full of them! I especially love when Jesus makes the miracle about the people doing the asking — the people wanting the miracle. He makes it about their belief. Their faith. In the above scripture references for example, he is telling them (and therefore, really, telling us) that we receive according to the degree of our faith. That means these folks had a role to play in these miracles. They had to believe that the conditions of their lives could be changed. They had to have a solid belief in that possibility.

Taking this a step further, if Jesus told us miracles can be done unto us according to our faith, doesn't that apply to everything, not just miracles? Miracles, good things, and even bad things? You know, things like... our knots — those "human muck" problems. Anything we experience — windfalls, setbacks, joys, sorrows, radiant health, sickness/disease, success, failure, etc. are all done unto us based on what we believe. Some of us find that to be a hard pill to swallow. But why? It sounds like a) exactly what Jesus taught and b) a fascinating key to life! We can influence and transform our lives in any way we wish, once we understand this concept as spiritual law.

When I am experiencing a problem, I try to stop and ask myself, "What am I believing, thinking, and expecting regarding this situation? What am I calling into my life here?" This is not an easy thing to do. In fact, I will let you in on a little secret: I fail at it pretty much every day. "What we believe" lies in our consciousness, our brains, the creative power of our mental nature. It's not an easy thing to have the self awareness to examine that. It's even harder to get a handle on the correlation between our beliefs and our life experience.

Ernest Holmes wrote in The Science of Mind®, "The whole teaching of Jesus was based on the theory that we are surrounded by an intelligent, Spiritual law, which does unto each as he believes. He implied the necessity of faith, conviction, and acceptance. That is, it must be measured out to us according to our own measuring. We must not only believe, we must know that our belief measures the extent and degree of our blessing. If our belief is limited, only a little can come to us, because that is as we believe."[1]

What do we believe? What lies in our consciousness? Our consciousness is the sum total of our thoughts and beliefs. Think of it this way: our consciousness creates a field around us, where we attract or repel our Good, our blessings, our own miracles. The Law of attraction would say that which is like unto itself is drawn. We are magnets attracting to us the essence of that which we are thinking and feeling. If we are putting out resentment, greed, hatred, fear... we draw more of that into our lives.

Divine Science puts it a little differently and calls it the Law of Expression. Because Spirit is all, you are one with Spirit, which is expressing in you, through you, and as you. Like produces like; that which is born of Spirit is Spirit.[2] Understanding, thinking, and speaking the truth of our unity and oneness with Spirit demonstrates the good we wish to see in our individual lives.

The good news is that we have the power to change our lives with our thoughts. We can guard our thoughts, accepting only the good. It is not easy, but it can be simple. Repel thoughts that deny your good — thoughts of sickness, fear, lack, failure. Focus solely on the good and believe it. This is something every single person can do. Jesus told us that. When the Centurion goes to Jesus, he tells him, I'm not worthy, only speak a word, and my servant will be healed! Only you can do it, Jesus (Matt. 8:5-13). But Jesus, the master teacher points out that, actually, it is done unto you as YOU believe. YOU can do it. The power is within you.

Recognizing this power within you is the way to create the life you want, claim your good, and live each day from this spiritual truth. If you are experiencing something burdensome, something heavy on your heart, I invite you to lay it down right now. Any belief in illness/disease, any sense of lack, feeling of isolation, any perceived problem. You can let it go. Don't claim it as your trouble, your issue, or your problem. Instead, I challenge you:

Claim the good in your life.
Claim the good for everyone you meet.
Claim wholeness, joy, abundance, freedom, and love. Declare, accept, and know that all is well, here and now.

A Word About That Word...

RECOGNIZING A UNIVERSAL GOD

"What if the person next to me tries to talk to me?"

This was my daughter's big concern, taking her first flight by herself at 19 years old. Funny how a conversation with a stranger can send a young adult into a full-blown panic. I told her the best way I knew to get a person on a plane to stop talking to you:

"Ask them if they want to talk about God."

While I was only joking, it does seem like nothing makes people more uncomfortable. For many, the word God itself can be a knee jerk, reactionary hot button. It can set people off, make them clam up, and irritate them. It brings out all kinds of emotions and opinions. For some people, God is a wonderful, positive, loving word. Lord help the person who tries that airplane trick on me — I would happily talk their ear off! We have all had our experiences with the G-word, good or bad, and we all attach our own value to it. As I like to say, "God is a tiny word with potentially BIG baggage." It is also, arguably, one of the richest words in existence.

My friend Wendy has called herself an atheist for most of her life. She tells me that deep down she is longing to believe in something, but she also admits that the word God makes her twitch. To her, saying she believed in God would be like saying she believed in a patriarchal Christian God, (her words) — a God outside of herself with some kind of external will over her life. That has never resonated with her or felt true. The semantics and meaning of the word God have always bothered her.

I pointed out to her that last time I checked, Christians don't own the word God. One particular religious group does not get to define God for all humanity. Far beyond the words, theologies, creeds, dogmas, and rituals of all religion lies the unlimited power, frequency, and energy of what I refer to as "God." I asked Wendy to consider changing the meaning of the word in her mind. If she didn't believe in God, what did she believe in?

This was her reply: "I believe in science, earth, the beauty of nature, life force energy, kindness, the power of positive thinking, and the power of my own belief in myself!" I just smiled because that all sounded great to me.

"Why can't all those things be God?" I asked her. She hadn't ever considered that.

If the word God brings you pain, confusion, or skepticism, I invite you to be brave enough to let go of semantics. Using the same word doesn't mean you accept and believe in "their" version of God (the one that might make you twitch.) It's okay to believe in your own meaning of the word. The word God need not be anthropomorphic, as if God is a person. It can simply embody high thoughts, deep truths, and meaningful wisdom. Two things to remember:

No one owns the word God.
You can create your own meaning for God.

Having said that, if you simply can't get past semantics, you can also use any other word you want. I often find religious words far too limiting. The more expansive, inclusive, universal, and all-encompassing the better, I say! As an Interfaith/New Thought minister, I have heard a LOT of them. When I say "God," in my books or sermons, please know that I am referring to the following concepts. All of them. Not one particular meaning, but all of them:

Absolute, All, Allah, Brahman, Buddha, Cause, Christ, Christ-Consciousness, Consciousness, Creator, Creation, Creative Force, Creative Process, Divine Being, Energy, Father, Frequency, God, Goddess, Good, Goodness, Holy Spirit, Infinite, Intelligence, Jehovah, Jesus, Light, Life, Life Force, Love, Mind, Mother, Mystery, Nature, One, Power, Principle, Providence, Reality, Source, Source of All, Spirit, Spirit of Life, Truth, Ultimate, Universe, Universal Presence*

*This is an incomplete list. Use what works for you!

Nearer Than Your Hands

UNITY WITH THE DIVINE

I am good friends with a married couple. The husband told me about a conversation he had recently with his wife. He was at work, and she was at home talking to him on her cell phone. During their long conversation, she said to him in an exasperated tone, "I can't find my phone. I've been looking for it everywhere!" She said that to him... *while on her cell phone.* Now, at this point, he had a couple choices. He could have said, "Um, you're on your phone, you nitwit." but he did not.

Instead, he feigned concern and said, "Really? Where did you have it last? Did you leave it in the bedroom?" (I forgot to mention; he thinks he's hilarious.) For a good ten minutes they discussed in all sincerity — while on the phone — all the possible places she could have left her phone. Finally, he suggested she check her hand. This woman is my friend, and I assure you she is perfectly intelligent. We've all had an embarrassing, face-palm, dingbat moment like that. That was just hers.

The story is a great illustration of God's truth. Her phone was there in her hand the whole time. There she was, spinning her wheels in a panic, searching, seeking, looking. Yet, in her seeking, she wasn't really noticing the truth of the situation. She was using her phone — using the very thing for which she was searching.

For many of us, that is what happens when we convince ourselves we should be actively seeking God. It has been said that we do not need to seek God because God is seeking us. Perhaps we just have to be willing to let ourselves be found. The creative process is happening around us, in us, and through us all the time. God is always there. As Alfred, Lord Tennyson said: "God is closer to you than breathing and nearer than your hands and feet" and I would add, WHETHER WE REALIZE IT OR NOT. It is the realization, the awareness of the God-Presence that is the key. And don't we feel silly sometimes when we finally realize it?

Like the fish who spends its whole life in search of this mystical, magical, "ocean" it keeps hearing about... *you're in it*! It is all around you. You don't have to do anything but accept that it is there and trust that it is what it is. What if, for this whole day, or just this moment, you completely believed and trusted this statement:

I am surrounded, supported, and loved.
My good is at hand.

Hurt by the Church

INTERFAITH/HONORING ALL PATHS TO GOD

I n my years working as a guest speaker and minister, I have been shocked by the number of people who have been somehow damaged or hurt by their religion, a particular church, or church leader. When I started to notice how common this was, it made me think back to my own story, to my specific experience with religion that ended up impacting my spiritual journey. I wouldn't go so far as to call it a faith crisis, but *faith setback* certainly applies. In the hopes that the old adage is true — that we learn and grow from hearing each other's stories, here's what happened to me.

In my mid-twenties, I was an unhappily married woman with two young babies, born back-to-back. My husband and I had been fighting a lot, struggling financially, and questioning our faith. We'd sought the help of a Christian marriage counselor, who ended up exhibiting some ethically questionable behavior. At one point, he invited us to his home to explore a multi-level marketing business opportunity, which should have been a big red flag — but hey, we were young and naive. It gets worse.

This same counselor invited us to his Bible-based, non-denominational Christian church. Now, that may seem innocent and well intentioned enough, but in hindsight, I suspect it fell into the category of behaviors that are discouraged by licensed marriage and family therapists. I don't know many professional marriage counselors who want to see their clients at church on Sunday, but I digress...

As I said, we were young and naive, and so, we went. It was there at this church that we got to know the minister, our marriage counselor's best friend. I won't even get into the part of the story where this minister tricked us — I mean "graciously loaned us"— the money for the down payment on our first house at a high level of interest without us clearly understanding the terms of the agreement. In hindsight, I truly cannot believe how young and naive we were. He, on the other hand, should have known better than to take advantage of young new church goers who viewed him as a person in a position of spiritual authority. I haven't even gotten to the faith setback yet.

The real problem came when I decided I had had enough, and I separated from my husband. As one would imagine, it was a very difficult time for all of us, and this minister invited me to a private lunch, just me and him. He placed his well-worn Bible on the restaurant table in between us. Finally! I thought, some personal ministering. Some spiritual help. A life line.

It was over twenty years ago, and I still remember him calmly asking me what was going on in my marriage that I felt I needed to divorce my husband and break up my family. So, I let loose. I described all kinds of disappointing behavior, irresponsibility, irreconcilability, unhappiness and utter misery — probably with an unnecessary amount of dramatic flair. The bottom line was, I was just too unhappy to stay married.

He didn't say anything for a long moment. He just nodded and chewed his food. Then he thoughtfully pushed his Bible across the table until it rested in front of me, and then he tapped it aggressively with his index finger.

"You show me where in here it says you deserve to be happy."

I blinked, confused.

Then he hit me with: "Where in the Word of God does it say you get to be *happy*?"

It sounded more like a thinly veiled threat than a question. He looked angry and aggressive in that moment. I remember feeling stupid and judged. I was angry right back at him, but I said nothing. It's not like I was so well versed in biblical theology that I had memorized scripture quotes ready to reference — nor would I have felt confident arguing my point to an ordained minister more than twice my age.

I didn't defend myself at all. I didn't question his spiritual authority (which in hindsight should have been questioned.) In fact, I think I nodded naively as if I understood his point and probably as if I were encouraging him to continue lecturing me about how divorce is wrong, God did not want me to do this, I was failing my children, and I was being selfish. I think I gave him the impression that I agreed with everything he said in the hopes it would make lunch end sooner.

I admit that my faith in God was young and immature at that time in my life, but that minister made me doubt whatever immature faith I had. I felt shamed and wrong, like I was doing Christianity wrong, like I was a failure. The truth is, I did not want to believe in a God that didn't care about my happiness. I did not want to choose a life of misery and unhappiness, walking around with a twisted opinion that God was fine with it all. There had to be more to life than that. There had to be more to God than that! The only thing that seemed clear to me was that I couldn't be a part of a church whose leadership instinct was to judge me and tell me how wrong I was.

I know now that the "problem" with this experience was that I genuinely believed in a different kind of God than that minister did. It was simply a difference in theological opinion, a difference in scriptural interpretation, a difference in life outlook. I believed back then as I do now, that God is Life. God is Harmony. God is Peace.

And God is Love. I believe this love flows through me and exists in me, as I co-create with God and manifest my best, happiest life. It took me many years to get comfortable with my beliefs, to find the principles and philosophy that work for me spiritually, to mature me into my current understanding of not only biblical scripture, but wisdom from the spiritual texts of many different faith traditions. I needed time to grow into the expanded consciousness I didn't even know I was seeking.

I wish I had had more spiritual understanding back then. I wish I could have told that minister that God does care about my happiness, that, "All things are possible to him who believes," and that includes my happiness (Mark 9:23). Looking back, I can see clearly that I didn't believe it was possible to find happiness with my husband. I take responsibility for that lack of belief. I didn't believe in our marriage, in our compatibility, or in our success. Surely that is at the very least *partly* to blame for the failure. I played a role in its demise because I wasn't praying from a place of "believing I had already received" the happiness I desired and deserved. Instead, I was believing in our incompatibility, focusing on negative thoughts, rehashing arguments in my mind, and imagining volatile conflicts—which in turn created more incompatibility, more negative thinking, more arguments, and more conflict. I was using spiritual law the wrong way—drawing to myself the exact things I didn't want. Without realizing it, I was creating my own pain, and I suffered because of it.

My experience with that particular minister pushed me away from Christianity for many years. Eventually, I found a loving faith community that accepted, supported, and sustained me for a long time. That church led to others, which led to more personal study and growth on my spiritual journey.

Most people I encounter who have these kinds of negative stories that impacted their journey end up not only okay, but often better off for the experience. Ironically, my own experience with that minister made me think more for myself spiritually, pray more, read the Bible more, and interpret things for myself. In a sense, he did me a favor because I could have easily turned into a miserable woman who checked her brain at the door of the sanctuary in order to blindly believe whatever the person in the pulpit told her to believe. Phew! Thank you, minister-man from my past, for saving me from *that* kind of life.

Experiences like this push us to recover, reconnect, and heal. If you are in a spiritual community or situation where it doesn't feel right, if it's painful or judgmental, or if it goes against what you know in your heart to be true of God, Spirit, Universe, Source, then seek God elsewhere, in another way. That is the best advice I have, however paltry it may be. When I tell people I honor all paths to God, I mean it. There are so many possibilities.

There is a path to God that works for you.
When you believe this, it appears.

I Spy With My Little Eye

OBSERVING THOUGHTS AND BELIEFS

Most of us would agree that human eyes are pretty important organs. I have a rudimentary understanding of what they do and how they work. Here's what I know for sure: our eyes make it so we can see. (Well, duh!) I figure if I can plug in my appliances and use them without really understanding how electricity works, maybe I don't need to know the complex anatomical workings of the eyes to enjoy their function. I open my eyes, I see. I'm grateful for this miraculous process of vision, as I'm sure you are, too.

I am very interested, however, in the spiritual meaning behind the eyes. Perhaps you have heard the saying, "The eyes are the windows of the soul." There is great debate about the origin of this quote, often attributed to William Shakespeare, Leonardo DaVinci, Ralph Waldo Emerson, John Milton, various English and French Proverbs, Jesus, and many others.

Jesus did teach us that, "The lamp of the body is the eye. If therefore your eye is good, your whole body will be full of light. But if your eye is bad, your whole body will be full of darkness. If therefore the light that is in you is darkness, how great is that darkness" (Matt. 6:22-23)! I have seen multiple translations of this scripture, using various words like: "... if your eye is *good*, if thine eye be *single*, if your eye be *clear*, or if your eye is *healthy*..." For me, the word *good* resonates. I like the idea of keeping my eyes focused on the goodness in life.

Many New Thought leaders believe that the eye symbolizes spiritual perception. When we look at, explore, or examine something, we are using our eyes to give our attention. What we give our attention to is what ends up influencing our lives, so it is so important to be aware of it. Our health and happiness are determined by what we focus on with not only our physical eyes, but with our mind's eye. How do we see with our mind's eye? With our perceptions, thoughts, beliefs, imagination, and visualizations. Jesus tells us that this is the key, if our "eye" is focused on good, our whole body will be full of light — meaning our experience will be good.

It sounds simple enough, but it's not always easy to focus on the good, perfect, power, and presence of God. We understand we should do this logically, but executing it in our everyday lives can prove challenging. Too often we are not focused only on the good. We try, but we complain, think negative thoughts, worry, imagine bad things happening, and visualize trouble in our lives. Intellectually, we believe in God as our one Source, the one Power — we see the amazing possibilities of faith! But we are human, and if we're honest about it, our faith is often riddled with doubt.

It is a natural human tendency to doubt our faith and get lost in our daily fears, worrying about things like not having enough money in the bank, potentially losing our job, or expecting loss. It's when we make the effort to circle back and refocus on our faith, not only our faith in God, but also our faith in spiritual law, that we recognize the good all around us. When we accept that the great spiritual essence of God is good and it is what this entire world is made up of — all people, all things, all experience — that's when we are "seeing with the single eye."

Here's the kicker: our free will gives us the choice. We can focus on the good (God) and have a trusting expectation of good experiences, or we can focus on the bad (our own negative thoughts and the darkness of our fears) and be filled with that great darkness! I believe it was Albert Einstein who said the most important decision we make is whether we believe we live in a hostile or friendly universe. What do you believe?

We know faith is a journey, and it takes commitment, reminding, practice, and daily effort. Seek the good in your life. Look for it, even when it's hard to find. Trust it is there, even when you can't see it physically — when you are up to your eyeballs in knots. Focus on the good when you do see it, especially in your mind's eye. Make this part of your daily spiritual practice.

Train your eye to be single and good,
and let your whole embodiment fill with light.

God Words

AFFIRMATIONS

W ords are important. We think them, read them, write them, and believe them, whether we realize it or not. As someone who reads a lot, writes a lot, and if I'm lucky, gets paid to speak words in public, I try to pay close attention to them. I generally read, write, and speak about one topic: God. I particularly like GOD WORDS because I believe they help us know our spiritual truth, understand who we are as children of the Divine, and reclaim our good.

What are God Words? Let me demonstrate with a quick exercise for you. It works best with real paper — even a sticky note is fine. Draw a line vertically down the middle of the paper so there are two columns.

On the top left column, write the words "God Is." Then, take a few minutes and describe the God of your understanding. Single words work best, nouns or adjectives — but there is no wrong answer. Just list the qualities of God. If you're like me, maybe you listed words like: (God is) Love, Peace, Joy, Power, Beauty, Everything, etc.

Now, on the top of the right column write the words, "I Am." I bet you think you're about to make a list of words that describe yourself. Nope, not yet. First, consider what the biblical reference is to the "I AM..."

Moses is told that "I Am that I Am" is the name of God (Exod. 3:14). Using "I Am" is how we realize our unity with God. If "I AM" is the name of God, then we are calling ourselves by the name of God in our daily usage of these words. "I" is our point of identification. When we use "I am," we are giving ourselves a quality or nature of being. We are quite literally using our word to claim a quality for ourselves. We can claim, "I am unlovable," or "I am sick," or "I am poor," but are those claims true to our divine nature? They are not.

Consider how Jesus used the "I Am" words to realize his unity with God, with statements such as: "I am the bread of life" (John 6:35). "I am the light of the world" (JOHN 8:12). "I am the way, the truth and the life" (John 14:6). It is our task to do the same, to affirm our individual unity with the Divine by speaking of our highest, best version of ourselves.

We know we are made in the likeness and image of our creator. When we describe our creator, we are really describing ourselves. Go back to your paper now, and look closely at all the words you chose to describe God. Take the time to copy each word that you wrote describing God and put it under "I Am." Say them out loud if you can. Sometimes it is difficult, or it feels weird or wrong.

For instance, if you wrote, "God Is Beauty" maybe you feel strange writing down or saying out loud, "I Am Beauty" (or even "I Am Beautiful.") The weirder the word feels, the more you should pay attention to it because it is TRUE. If you wrote, "God is Patient," you may think you are not patient at all. But the truth is, the potential of that God quality of patience certainly lies within in you. How can it not? You're a child of God. All potential is there!

We can use the words "I am" followed by God Words to define all the potential good that we are capable of, declaring the highest version of who we are. What you end up with is a list of simple affirmations. Affirming these words as a fact, proudly, in the present tense, from a place of power helps us understand and align with our spiritual truth. It may take some time practicing these affirmations, looking at them, and thinking about them before we really believe them, and that's okay. It's called spiritual practice for a reason. When we affirm something often enough, our subconscious mind starts to act on what we are saying, producing results far beyond our imagination.

God Words are Good Words.
Think about them often.
Read them.
Write them.
Affirm them.
Believe them.

Using the Magic Words

UNITY WITH THE DIVINE

Previously, we did an exercise where we described the characteristics of God, in order to understand more about ourselves and our divine qualities. We used these words to write simple affirmations and become more aligned with our spiritual truth. Let's look at God's characteristics more deeply, as we explore more ways we can use these words in our spiritual practice to reclaim and reveal our good.

New Thought leaders Fannie James and Malinda Cramer, who wrote the Divine Science Principles and Practice text, described in detail what they believed to be "The Inherencies of God." Inherency means: "the state of being a fixed characteristic" — in this case, a fixed characteristic of God. They noted the inherencies of God as: Wisdom, Knowledge, Understanding, Power, Life, Joy, and Love.[1] In addition, there are accepted qualities of God, such as: Peace, Beauty, Truth, Order, Harmony, etc., all lovely "God-Words."

To be clear, these inherencies and qualities are just that — *words*. Humans often use language to understand God because that is all we have to work with, but I do think it's important to note that words can never fully describe and label something as incredible and inherently indescribable as God! But we can certainly try. In our trying, our seeking, and our studying, we discover these Divine, inherent characteristics and traits.

Having said all that, these inherencies are amazing, wonderful, magical words. To me, the true power behind them is the fact that they are tools we can use in our spiritual practice. They aren't just words to describe God, they are our inherent nature as children of the Divine. Consider the bold statement:

What is true of God is true of ME.

The inherencies of God are the truth that we turn to when we need spiritual support, and when we wish to offer support to others. They are the words on which we can choose to focus and meditate. When spoken into our prayers, these words align us with the power of Spirit. When I am feeling troubled, I can compassionately ask myself, "What is the Divine quality, the trait, the inherency of God that I desire to recognize in my life? — That I wish to realize? What is the God-Truth I would like to be revealed here in this situation?" Getting to the root of that helps dissolve what I call the "human muck" of our lives, (a.k.a. our *knots!*) the human conditions and experiences that are less than desirable and in need of change.

Meditating on, praying about, and affirming our true nature helps shut out anything that may feel contrary to it. Meditating on the specific inherency of which we are needing a realization eventually brings the truth of it into our consciousness. I don't mean to be trite when I describe this process as magical; I believe it is.

For instance, when I am experiencing illness or disease, I desire *harmony* and *intelligence* in my physical body's expression. When I am lonely, I need to realize the truth of the Divine *love* and *joy* unfolding in my life. When I am experiencing failure at work, I know what I am really seeking is *wisdom* and *power*. If my finances appear to be lacking, I need only realize the natural *abundance* and *prosperity* flowing all around me. Using my consciousness, I can take the time to be still, affirm, and know those truths, for myself, and for all beings. These inherencies of God are critical to our spiritual work and our spiritual practice.

We inherit these attributes because we are all children of God.
They are our gifts to use and reclaim our good.

Magic Spiritual Glasses

UNITY WITH ALL LIFE

D id you know that some people identify as color blind, and
color blindness is considered an actual disability? In
researching this, I learned that it's not even called color blindness
because it is technically not blindness. It is called color vision
deficiency. It is also not one condition; it is a range of conditions,
from mild to severe. It is a rare disability in that for many who have it,
not for all, but for many, there is a way to temporarily fix it. Specially
tinted lenses can help a person with color vision deficiency see colors
more accurately. Forgive me for oversimplifying, but to me, they
seem like magic glasses.

I have seen videos of this scenario on social media. If you've never
seen one — google "color blind glasses" and the various videos will
pop up. Here's how it works. Usually it is a grown man (because
color deficiency effects men more than women.) It is often a dad or a
grandpa who has had this condition his whole life, and the family is
gathered around outside on their birthday or Father's Day or
sometimes Christmas. The men are always presented with a pair of
these glasses as a gift. The same wonderful, feel-good thing happens
every time. The men put on the glasses, look around, become

emotional, and start crying. They are often completely overcome with emotion.

Why? Because for their whole life, they didn't know what they weren't seeing. They did not know how beautiful all the color expressions were. It's shocking to them, to see the beauty and fullness of Life revealed in an instant. I feel like that is worth thinking about for a moment. Do you recognize the beauty in all people, all life, all the time? Of course not. We know we should, and we probably try. But sometimes, we can't or just plain don't want to see the God in everyone.

How do we see what we don't know we aren't seeing? We don't know what we don't know we don't know, right? How do we fix that? What are the "magic spiritual glasses" we can put on to see the Divine in everyone, to see everyone's talents, and colorful unique expressions — and get to a place of celebrating them? Magic spiritual glasses do not exist, but it is clear that our work begins and ends in our conscious awareness.

How do we see as God sees? My best answer is: we ask for help. I think sometimes those who study New Thought principles, fully believing that true spiritual power is within, forget that we can still ask for help. We may not believe in duality and separation from the Divine. We may not pray to a God in the sky in a beseeching way, but that doesn't mean we can't still use our spiritual practice to ask for help. Let us ask affirmatively, through spiritual mind treatment to be shown what we aren't seeing:

As I become aware of the one Power, one Infinite Intelligence, that simply IS, I recognize this power as the goodness of Spirit. This goodness of Life is ever and always expressing in and through all creation. This includes me, and my being, and my life, and it includes all people, all beings, all life.

The nature of God's creation is one of diversity. As I look around, I begin to really notice that the colorful differences I see are all forms of Source. There is always something and someone to recognize as the goodness of God. I look for these opportunities more and more. I take

*every opportunity to see the harmony of God in and through all things...
all people, no matter the expression. I claim this right here, right now,
that this is what my eyes behold — the complete and perfect in all
creation. There is nothing else to see; I know only harmony, unity, and
oneness through all possible individualizations.*

*I am so grateful for all the things I see and am yet to see because I
know the truth of their beautiful, colorful perfection. I accept and
welcome this shift in consciousness. It is with great joy that I release this
into the action of the law, declaring it as good and very good. And So
It Is.*

*There is good to be found all around you.
Ask for it to be revealed, and then look for it,
believing you will see.*

Have an Epiphany

TUNING IN TO GUIDANCE

Buried deep beneath all my religious training, I'm a "hippy woo-woo" kind of gal. Therefore, I have always had a soft spot for the Christian story of Epiphany because of all the "new age" type spiritual elements sprinkled throughout it. Found in the second chapter of the Gospel of Matthew, the story explains King Herod's outrage over the birth of Jesus and the journey of the wisemen, traveling to visit the newborn baby. Herod insisted they find the baby for him, so that he too could go worship Jesus. Oh, the irony. (Can you really call yourself a wise man if you believe for a second that Herod ever intended to bow down and worship the new King Jesus?)

Nevertheless, the wisemen leave Herod and begin their journey. The star, which they had seen in the East, went before them until it stood where the baby was (Matt. 2:9). It seems like simple Sunday school trivia for children. Question: "How did the wisemen find baby Jesus?" Answer: "They followed the star." Okay, but how often do we stop and think about the mystery of that guidance? God, needing a way to communicate with the wisemen, a way to lead them to the place they needed to be, used a beautiful shining star in the sky as a sign for them to see and follow. We accept that this was a logical, feasible way for God to send a message to those men over 2,000 years ago.

But perhaps the deeper question is, is it still a logical and feasible method of divine communication today? Most of us cringe, and say no way, that following the stars and paying attention to astrology in general is slightly less than "holy." How often do we give others flak for seeking and believing in signs and guidance from the stars, even if they believe it is truly guidance from God? It's a fine line that gets both blurred and regularly stomped on these days.

I have read some interesting "planetary" explanations for human behavior in my lifetime. I will admit to finding the occasional astrological forecast to be at the very least thought provoking. I have even experienced a random revelation or two during a new moon, full moon, or eclipse. Who am I to say God isn't still using the stars to guide people? We have all probably witnessed a shooting star, seen a brightly shining planet, experienced the vast expansiveness of the Milky Way sky and been deeply moved and spiritually inspired. Or is that just me?

Later in the Epiphany story, the scripture slips in some subtle references to dream interpretation, another "new age" type detail I find myself quick to embrace. "Then, being divinely warned in a dream that they should not return to Herod, they departed for their own country another way" (Matt. 2:12). The wisemen receive a warning message in their dreams from God, not to return to Herod. And then the scripture tells us that an angel appeared to Joseph in a dream, saying, "Arise, take the young Child and His mother, flee to Egypt, and stay there until I bring you word; for Herod will seek the young Child to destroy Him" (Matt. 2:13).

These people — Joseph and the wisemen — received a message from God in their dreams. Does that mean people today (regular people like you and me) can receive such powerful messages from God about our lives? In his book, *God's Message to the World: You've Got Me All Wrong*, Neale Donald Walsch suggests that God has always guided and talked directly to human beings. He presents an amazing interfaith laundry list of examples such as Lao Tzu, Buddha, Moses, Jesus, Muhammad, Mother Mary, Teresa of Avila, Joan of Arc, and many others who communicated with and were inspired by the Divine.[1]

He further asserts that perhaps all of us are being spoken to, every minute, every hour, every day. He presses us to consider whether divine communication is still happening today. How would you respond if you walked into work and your coworker declared God spoke to him in a dream? Many of us would say (or at least think), "No way!" just like we would say finding guidance and signs in the stars and astrology is also a no way. But can we really know for sure?

A prophet is someone who receives and transmits a message from God to the world. Countless religions are built upon not only a particular prophet, but the subsequent message. God uses all sorts of things (even stars and dreams) to reach humans. Believing in the omnipotent power of God, this makes perfect sense! The more still we become, the easier it is for us to be guided, the more signs, symbols, and intuitive knowing we receive. The more aligned we are with Spirit, the easier it is to understand God's will for our highest good and best life.

Epiphany means "the unveiling" or "the revealing," from the Greek word *epiphaneia*, meaning manifestation or appearance. The wisemen were the first to recognize the newborn child as divine love in expression, God incarnate in physical form, the Presence of Eternal Good. They may also have been the first to realize that what they experienced must be available not just for them, but for all people. The Goodness of God is available for all of us to realize, every day, every hour, every moment.

How open are you to experiencing your own epiphany? Are you ready and willing to receive your own guidance and inspiration from the Infinite Intelligence in a different, unique, or unusual way? Don't be afraid to follow the stars and embrace your dreams!

Remember, Spirit uses any resource available to reach us because Spirit is limitless, and all things are possible.

Gratitude Games

GRATITUDE

Everyone knows gratitude is a powerfully effective spiritual practice, but if we are honest — it's also the one we tend to blow off and most easily forget. We might make a gratitude list now and then, or start a gratitude journal, but eventually, we get bored and move on. Some creative ways to incorporate more gratitude into your daily habits might be: giving thanks before meals, making an effort to say thank you to the people you encounter, or simply giving thanks for the abundance of air available for you to breathe. One of my favorite ways to use gratitude is a game I like to play when I wake up every day. It goes like this:

First thing in the morning, before you get out of bed, think of five things for which you are truly grateful. Don't get out of bed until you do it. You don't have to write them down or spend an hour thinking about them. Just make the list in your head, and really thank God for these blessings. Try doing it every day for a week with no repeated answers. That's tricky — you may have to get creative! For me, it starts to feel like a game and a challenge to start my day saying thank you to the God presence within me. I have noticed I get out of bed with a smile a lot more often!

Another way to use gratitude in your spiritual practice is to give thanks for things you have not yet received. How is that even possible? It's about becoming aligned with the feeling and frequency in your consciousness. Think of it as a creative form of visualization, where you are living so deeply in the place of your desired outcome that you are already grateful for the demonstration. This could involve journaling it — literally writing down, "Thank you God, Spirit, Source, for _____ , or something better." (I always add "or something better" to my journaling because I would never want to put a limit on Spirit, nor would I want to limit my good.) Keep in mind this isn't only for material objects, but anything for which we can be grateful, like good health, a happy relationship, or a new job opportunity.

Another unusual but effective way to use gratitude is to be thankful for bad things. That sounds ridiculous, right? Surely it's a typo, and she meant to say *good things*? Why would we be grateful for the difficult, horrible, frustrating moments we experience in life — those gross *knots* we want undone? For the same reason that sometimes during a dark and stormy day, we realize how much we enjoy the sunshine. Encountering darkness helps us appreciate the light.

Where in your life can you look back and see that some horrible thing you experienced was actually something for which you can be grateful? For instance...

- Maybe that terrifying health diagnosis, as scary and awful as it was, made you change your habits and take better care of your body.
- Perhaps that abusive relationship you were in for years helped you learn to respect and value yourself, teaching you about the kind of loving, healthy relationship you deserve.

- Maybe the boss that made you miserable at that job you really hated motivated you to follow your dream to go back to school.
- Perhaps that time in your life when you could barely make ends meet made you more compassionate and giving toward those less fortunate.

When I think about my "rock bottom" years, when I was a freshly divorced single mother, lacking job skills, barely surviving financially, feeling utterly lost and miserable, I was definitely not grateful. I wouldn't want to go back to that period in my life for anything, *but*, I do know that if it were not for those difficult things I experienced, I would not have ended up on the spiritual path that led me to where I am today. That chaotic time in my life motivated me to become a spiritual seeker. I sought a better life for myself, and I needed to learn spiritual practices to do it.

All those difficult moments motivated me to take practical steps to manifest my highest good. It turns out I got so interested in it, that now I teach other people how to do that, too. Today, I am grateful that seemingly bad life experiences in the past put my career on a trajectory that now includes teaching, ministry, motivational speaking, and writing.

Maybe you've blown off or forgotten about gratitude as a spiritual practice. Is it time to revisit it? Can you take gratitude out of your spiritual toolbox and play with it today?

Gratitude is always there,
waiting for you to become aware of it.

The Spiritual Bread Fight

INTERFAITH/HONORING ALL PATHS TO GOD

I recently asked my husband to stop at the store on his way home from work and pick up some bread. Picture a loaf of bread right now in your mind. Hold onto that picture for just a second.

Later that evening, he waltzed into the house with a long, skinny French baguette inside a fancy white sleeve of bakery paper. He set it on the counter along with a couple other items he had bought and then started systematically putting things away. I squinted at the baguette and tipped my head like a confused little puppy. What I wanted and needed was a loaf of store bought, pre-sliced, boring old white-or-wheat-doesn't-matter, wrapped in a clear plastic bag with a twist-tie *bread*. The kind of bread a kid would use to make a peanut butter and jelly sandwich for their school lunch. No one makes a peanut butter and jelly sandwich with a French baguette. What the heck was this guy thinking?

At this point in our relationship, we had been together as a couple for more than ten years, but something about him bringing home this crusty baguette made me want to rethink things. How could he not instinctively know what we needed? How could he not know what I meant when I said, "Pick up some bread?" How could he misunderstand such simple directions? Did he really think I meant a fancy, crusty French baguette? Is that what he pictured in his mind?

"I said *bread*," was all I could spit out. I suspect my irritation and outrage were not well hidden.

He gave a pathetic shrug, no doubt realizing his mistake, and dug in his heels. "What? Is that not bread?"

Well of course it was bread, but at that point I was more interested in beating him with it than trying to make him understand how wrong he was. That crust though... *ouch*. I stumbled through the explanation that I wanted regular sandwich bread, the kind we go through every week like normal sandwich making people. He dug his heels in further and said I'd have to deal with it. I, being the cool-headed, ever spiritually aware person, walked away from the argument.

But the whole misunderstanding got me thinking...

If a word like bread could be so misunderstood, so misconstrued, and lead to such frustration, anger, and disappointment, surely a word like God could cause a lot more trouble. Even between people who seemingly love each other like we do. God is a tiny word with potentially BIG baggage. The real root of the "bread" problem was this: what he graciously brought home from the store was a) not what I wanted and b) not at all what I needed. I couldn't do what I wanted with that version of bread he brought home. He messed up my plans, and that is what irritated me.

I sometimes wonder if it's the same with God. Everybody has their own particular version of God. If I asked 100 people to picture God in their minds, everyone would be imagining vastly different ideas. For instance, my version of God is a universal loving power present in our human consciousness. She is found in a blanket of stars, the ocean waves, a colorful sunset, as much as he is found in the ancient wisdom texts, churches, synagogues, temples, and ashrams. It's what I connect with through meditation and prayer, and it's what I consciously co-create with in my life, through affirmations and positive self-talk. That's the version of God I use, the version with which I make my sandwich for my daily lunch.

I have friends though, very good friends in fact, who enjoy getting out the giant serrated knife needed to carve out a crusty piece of their "French baguette" version of God. They might read from a certain holy book, sing two-hundred-year-old hymns, or take part in sacred rituals whose meanings are totally lost on me. I can't always do much with their "French baguette" style God. We still eat together though and get delightfully fat together on our versions of the same thing: bread (God.)

We don't force feed each other and insist our version of God is the only correct one. We don't present our versions to each other and say, "deal with it." In fact, most of my friends like getting together to sample each other's God offerings. We chat about the things we find weird, awesome, and different. We say things like, "Wow! This is so interesting! I love that this is so meaningful to you..." and "I've never thought about God in this way — I love it!" We talk and laugh and think and grow spiritually. We are respectful and kind, and I'm grateful for that. It feels like we are one community of seekers, individually discovering the best parts of God that work for us personally and generously sharing those morsels with each other.

It reminds me of a beautiful poem by Rumi called "One One One."

The lamps are different
But the light is the same.
So many garish lamps in the dying brain's lamp-show,
Forget about them.
Concentrate on the essence, concentrate on the Light.
In lucid bliss, calmly smoking off its own holy fire,
The Light streams towards you from all things,
All people, all possible permutations of good, evil, thought,
*   passion.*
The lamps are different,

but the Light is the same.
One matter, one energy, one Light, one Light-mind,
Endlessly emanating all things.
One turning and burning diamond,
One, one, one.
Ground yourself, strip yourself down,
To blind loving silence.
Stay there, until you see
You are gazing at the Light
With its own ageless eyes.

Perhaps God is the truth that transcends all versions of itself, all manner of tradition. I believe God is ultra-personal to humanity, in the most universal sense, and I'm going to go out on a limb and say that is what really matters. I also can't help but be reminded that we "cannot live by bread alone..."

In case you were wondering, my husband went back to the store for me that night and got me the bread I wanted because he's actually a very nice person. If you find someone who does things like this for you in a relationship, keep them. If you find friends who encourage you to experience your own version of God and are the least bit interested in sharing theirs with you, keep them, too.

In our simple willingness to be open to all versions of God,
we show our willingness to receive the unlimited versions of our good. Be
kind, be open, be willing.

Expect Good Things

OBSERVING THOUGHTS AND BELIEFS

Prayer is a big part of most people's faith. What we may not realize is, our everyday words and our moment-to-moment thoughts are always our prayers. The Infinite Intelligence of God is not *only* listening when we bow our heads and fold our hands in deliberate prayer. We are creative beings, just like our creator Mother-Father God. The way God works through us is with the words we speak over our lives and what we believe and affirm for ourselves. We often don't want to examine, much less take responsibility for, what we're really "putting our faith in."

In his book, *How to Develop the Faith that Heals*, Fenwicke Holmes defines faith as: "a confident attitude of expectancy."[1] It reminds us not only that faith and attitude are closely associated, but also that our expectations matter. I am inclined to take his definition a step further and describe faith as: a confident expectancy of GOOD. So often we think of faith in big, vague terms: Our faith in God, our faith in Jesus, Christian belief, belief in any particular faith tradition, our belief in ritual, ceremony, our belief in the church as an institution, etc. but... faith is really just our belief in general. Our belief in anything! Our belief about ourselves, other people, or how the world works. What we believe about relationships, money, love, work. Faith is what we think will happen. It is what we *expect* will happen.

Jesus told us, "According to your faith, be it done to you," (Matt. 9:29) and "When you pray, believe you have received it, and you shall receive" (Mark 11:24). We know these words of Jesus are true whether we apply them positively or negatively. This is spiritual law. We can walk around believing bad things will happen and thinking our life is a hot mess, and we receive exactly what we believe. We wind up experiencing knots. It is always worth exploring and examining what we truly believe about our lives. It is spiritually powerful work.

When you understand that faith is a confident expectancy of good, it begs the question: Are you expecting good? Are you expecting good things to come into your life? Do you expect good things to happen? If you are anything like me, sometimes you do, and sometimes, you don't. But the best part is, we can always change our thoughts and beliefs and reevaluate what we are putting our faith in.

I don't mean to gloss over how challenging this can be! Let's be honest, sometimes in life we experience knots that are outright painful and difficult — hardships, illness, loss. So, what do we do in the midst of them? We must remember the difference between FACTS and TRUTH. They are two different things. Think of FACTS as... the conditions of our life. Outward appearances. The manifested effects of our thought. TRUTH (capital T-Truth) is a Divine Reality, it is what God, Spirit, the Universe intends for us. It is our Divine nature. It is true and unchangeable, whether we are experiencing it in our current conditions or not.

Jesus saw beyond conditions all the time. He denied them; he saw and claimed what was perfect and True. It's how he performed miracles. Our great goal is to emulate the master! Jesus represents man's potentiality, sent to teach us about our inherent connection to God's goodness. It is our birthright because we are all God's children. Sometimes we have to let go of our belief in the negative things going on in our lives, and regardless of appearances, trust and believe completely in that goodness of God. That is faith — that confident expectancy of good.

So, for example, A FACT might be symptoms you are experiencing, or a diagnosis of a disease, but the TRUTH is the perfect health, wholeness, and balance that God created you with and intends for you. A fact might be that you are fighting with your spouse and not getting along... but the Truth is that you both have within you God's radical, unconditional love that you receive and express freely. See the difference? Divine Truth is what we know deep down to be Real... Even when we can't quite see it. On which one do you want to focus? In which one do you want to put your FAITH? Focusing on a negative fact, on a condition that can change, is NOT having an expectancy of Good.

Ernest Holmes, (Fenwicke's brother) wrote in *The Science of Mind®*, "Let us seek the good and the true and believe in them with our whole heart, even though every man we meet may be filled with suffering, and limitation appears at all sides. We cannot afford to believe in imperfection for a single second, to do so is to doubt God."
2

In our darkest, most difficult moments,
we cannot afford to believe in limitation.
What are you putting your faith in today?
Have an expectancy of good!

Be Still

W hat do you think of when you hear the words: BE STILL? I think of Psalm 46:10...

"Be still and know that I am God."

It's one of my favorites, and it is displayed in my living room on a big wooden plaque. I am sure it has different meanings and interpretations, but for me, it is simply a reminder of how important it is to be still, calm, and quiet, in order to become aware of and know the presence of God. Moments of stillness are rare these days, yet they are so valuable to our spiritual life. Practicing stillness builds trust. When is the last time you truly became still and asked for guidance, then stayed still long enough to receive an answer? I would remind you that: Spirit within never fails to respond when we ask from a place of believing and trusting in our unity with It. It never fails.

Not long ago, something happened that I think beautifully illustrates this idea. First, you should know a little fun fact about me: I love birds. I love watching birds, and I love feeding birds. So, naturally, I have a bunch of bird feeders around the outside of my house, including a hummingbird feeder out back on our patio. They love it.

What happens though, is sometimes the little guys get confused. If we leave our garage door up, they think they're headed under the patio toward the feeder, but they accidentally go into our garage and they get stuck. This has happened at least four times over the past couple of years. (You would think we'd just learn to shut the garage door!) The other night, as we were walking a friend out to her car, sure enough there was a hummingbird flitting around our garage, crying and squeaking. If you have never heard a hummingbird cry, it's the saddest, most pitiful little squeak you've ever heard.

Do you know how to solve the problem of a hummingbird stuck in your garage? There is a very specific trick to it. I know all about it. All I needed was a rake. A regular old yard rake that I would use to collect leaves. I slowly lifted the rake up to where the bird was flitting around, and I held it there as still as I possibly could. Eventually, the hummingbird got on the rake and perched there. Seriously. He did it. I have no idea why, but it is magical and exhilarating to watch it happen.

Now, I wasn't done. I then had to very... very... slowly lower the rake and carry the bird on the rake out of the garage. This was not an easy process. It took about 10-15 tries because if I moved too fast and I tried to rush the matter, the bird would get spooked and fly off the rake, back up into the garage, and I would have to start the process all over again. But eventually, after keeping at it, the hummingbird stayed on long enough and aligned with the rake. It trusted the rake, it trusted me holding the rake, and the bird was led exactly where it needed to go.

I'm sure you are sensing the analogy here. Do you know how hard it is for a hummingbird to be completely still? Unless they stop to drink sugar water, they almost never stop flying! It goes against its very nature to be still. But the little guy did it... because he wanted some guidance. He needed guidance and help. In many ways it goes against OUR nature to be still. We humans love to flit about with our ideas and our egos and our busyness, don't we? I encourage you to take time to BE STILL, in whatever way works for you, whether it be sitting in silence, meditating, praying, or just taking some time to be alone and thinking about Spirit.

Trust Spirit will show you exactly what you need to get in alignment. Let Spirit lead you exactly where you need to go.

Go Higher

OBSERVING THOUGHTS AND BELIEFS

While I was preaching once, a gentleman in the congregation raised a prayer request for a mass shooting that had happened earlier that week. He offered prayers for the victims and everyone involved in that tragedy.

But what got to me was what he said after that. I think he spoke for many people in this country who are frustrated that these tragedies have become commonplace. He mentioned that it was starting to feel like no place is safe anymore, and it made him not want to attend gatherings in public places. He said he was struggling because he knew that God is our refuge, our safety and security, but... he was still feeling what I would call a legitimate fear.

We do know that God is our refuge. Psalm 46 reminds us of that, "God is our refuge and strength, A very present help in trouble. Therefore we will not fear..."

But we do.

That is not a judgement; it is a pretty normal human reaction. We are human, and here is something I never dreamed that I would ever write in a book: we are also sinners. It makes me twitch to write that, so stick with me here. What I mean by that, is that we sometimes don't think the way God wants us to think.

"To Sin" literally means to miss the mark, to miss the point, like an archer who misses the target. So, when we sin, we are off track. We have missed God's point for living. We have perhaps missed God altogether.

There is quite a bit of evidence that these are scary times in which we are living. When we focus on those scary, fear-inducing conditions instead of focusing on God being our refuge, God being our safety and security, God being the One Source of Love... we are sinning. Ugh. Great. What can we do about that?

There are so many ways to react to these tragic events that keep happening over and over. We can get angry, we can be so afraid we don't want to leave the house, we can judge and blame others, we can get depressed and feel defeated. While those are all legitimate ways to react, ways that nobody is really going to argue with, they don't feel very good when we choose them. Deep down, we know they don't jive with the love and joy that God wants us to experience in life.

One of our knee-jerk reactions to a negative news report, such as when there is a mass shooting, is to resist it. We complain about these horrible acts, we talk about them, we declare our outrage and fear! (Rightly so.) The problem is that when we resist "evil," we give it our attention and continue to make it real. We know that what we give our attention to creates our experience. We must be careful not to argue for our fears by discussing them too emphatically. Have you ever heard that saying, "What we resist, persists?"

Imagine you heard a warning on the news about an increase in crime in your area. You might decide to put bars on the windows of your home, install security cameras, and get a weapon to protect yourself. You might even become suspicious of anyone you don't recognize. Your neighbor, however, didn't see the warning on the news. She is as friendly as ever, happily unaware of the supposed threat. She makes no changes to her home and has no reason to believe she needs protection. One response isn't wrong, nor is the other necessarily right. The spiritually aware response would perhaps draw from both places — simultaneously acknowledging that yes, there may be crime in the area, but also choosing to live without fear taking over your thoughts, beliefs, and decisions. To hold a consciousness of contentment and well-being is part of having faith.

Many contemporary New Thought leaders genuinely suggest not watching the news at all, and certainly not at night right before we go to sleep. The idea behind this is that you do not want any negativity, any violence, any tragedy, any sense of evil to enter your Divine consciousness, which is actively focused on love, light, Truth, and God. It is a perfectly fine suggestion, and if you practice this and it's working for you–GREAT!

I did it myself for several years, but I stopped because I felt like I was missing out on an important opportunity. I was losing the chance to view tragic world events as a prayer request. When awful tragedies happen, I have the opportunity to pray and affirm what I know to be True of God and God's world, even if it does not seem true because of what's happened.

If I see a story about a mass shooting, or terrorist attack, or some other hate-filled awful thing, I have the option to go within and affirm peace, harmony, and love. My words and thoughts are powerful, and I believe each one of us has the opportunity to be an instrument of peace, sending peaceful thoughts to people all over the world who need them. Violence is a cycle that can only be broken when we consciously refuse to engage or participate in it.

We can use the opportunity to affirm the opposite "God word," and be an expression of that. For instance, if there is hatred in the world, I know God is Love, and therefore, I am Love. If there is sadness, God is Joy, and I am an expression of that Joy. And in this case, if there is violence, I know God is Peace, and I am peaceful.

We can make a conscious decision not to lower ourselves, lower our thinking, lower our energy when these things happen. Instead, we can go higher to our refuge in God. A beautiful lesson in the mystical text of Judaism called the Kabbalah says, "The falls of our life provide us with the energy to propel ourselves to a higher level." In other words, when world events go violent and low, we go can always go higher, to what we know to be true of God.

May our spiritual understanding lift and lead us higher,
to our greatest experience of our good.

How Do You Pray?

PRAYER

When I was about 15 years old, my great Aunt Charlotte came to visit from the other side of the country. She was my father's aunt, and even though I was told I had known her when I was younger, I didn't really remember her. The visit was fun. She was a chatty, charming, witty old woman in her 80s, standing just over 5 feet tall, with curly grey hair, thick glasses, and a raspy old lady voice that got raspier when she laughed. She reminded me of Sophia Petrillo from the Golden Girls without the bamboo purse.

The most interesting thing happened during Aunt Charlotte's visit. She was staying in the guest room down the hall from my room, and one night, she went to bed before I did. While walking past her room, I noticed her door was ajar. I peeked in and saw something fascinating. Aunt Charlotte was praying. She was kneeling on the floor (no small feat at her age) with her elbows resting on the bed, her hands clasped together, eyes closed, and she was whispering softly. I froze for a moment in the hallway, listening, watching. I couldn't look away. It was simultaneously the weirdest and most adorable thing I had ever seen! My great Aunt Charlotte was praying like a little child.

A million thoughts ran through my head as I tiptoed on to my room. Did she always pray that way, kneeling on the floor? Had she prayed that way her entire life? Did she pray like that in church? Did she even go to church? I had never prayed that way. Was that bad? Was I lazy because I never got down on my knees? Was she doing it right and I had I been doing it wrong? Was there a "right way" to pray? An epiphany began to emerge in my naive teenager brain: People pray in different ways!

I did not get any answers to my internal questions because I certainly wasn't going to voice them, but I suspect my wondering all those years ago played a role in me becoming an interfaith minister some twenty plus years later. I have learned a few things since then: 1) Prayer is a very private, personal spiritual practice. 2) People really do pray in all kinds of ways — and none of them are necessarily right or wrong. And 3) Sometimes... people do not want to talk about how they pray. (Refer back to number 1.)

The Bible discusses how to pray rather clearly. Jesus instructs us in Matthew 6:6, "... when you pray, go into your room, and when you have shut your door, pray to your Father who is in the secret place..." (That must have been Aunt Charlotte's mistake — she left that door to her room open!) Jesus is explaining that prayer takes place in private, when we go within and use our mind and our thoughts to communicate with God. This is not to say we can't speak our prayers out loud. He also reminds us that our Father knows the things we need before we ask Him, and he tells us to pray what is commonly known as the Lord's Prayer (Matt. 6:8-13).

The guidance and Divine wisdom of Jesus with regard to prayer is wonderful information, and for some, it is a good starting point. I am the last person to tell anyone how they should pray. I have seen people pray on their knees, wailing in tears. I have seen people pray lying down in silence to the point I thought they were sleeping. I have heard prayers chanted and recited by a group in unison. I have heard and been moved by songs of prayer, sung by choirs. It seems to me whatever instructions we are given about prayer can be interpreted in any number of ways.

In fact, I am tempted to make a sweeping declaration: It doesn't matter how you pray; it only matters that you do. Why? Because prayer is powerful and effective. Numerous studies have proven that groups of people who prayed for sick people actually helped them recover faster than those who were not prayed for. As I recall, one of the most famous involved almost 400 hospitalized cardiac patients in the early 1980's. While I am tremendously oversimplifying the results, the double-blind study showed that the patients that received prayer generally turned out healthier.

Keep in mind the study did not specify the WAY in which a participant prayed, but merely that they prayed. Eyes closed or open — doesn't matter. Contemplative, affirmative, thanksgiving, intercession, centering prayer — doesn't matter. Silent, spoken out loud, whispered softly — doesn't matter. Crossed legged, lying down, standing, sitting, or kneeling by the bed in your nightgown like dear Aunt Charlotte — doesn't matter.

Prayer is powerful because we (the faithful, the spiritual, the consciously aware) each tap into our own way of doing it. Even though it may feel awkward, I encourage you to talk in your families, with your neighbors and your friends about how you pray. Share your spiritual practice freely! We can learn from each other and be open to new ways of seeking the kingdom within and communicating with the Divine. But ultimately, we will do what works for us. That is the beauty of God, for God is multifaceted and unlimited.

God expresses through each of us in different ways,
including all the ways in which we pray.

When We Forget to Heal

RECOGNIZING HEALTH AND WHOLENESS

I recently suffered an accident. It was bloody and painful. Oh, and very stupid. I was doing the dishes, like I do every night. The sink was full of hot soapy water and dirty cups, plates, pans, and silverware, like usual. I put my hand in to reach for the next item, and WOW! Somebody must have put a machete in the sink because next thing I knew, my finger had a huge, jagged cut across it, and there was blood running down my hand.

There was a lot of squealing, but I'm proud to say that I did not cry. I thought I needed stitches for sure. Turns out it stopped bleeding after about five minutes, and I just needed a band aid. But it was so deep! There was so much blood! It was so jagged! The throbbing! I was pretty convinced this cut was going to hurt for days.

I went to bed that night, and guess what? The next morning, I had forgotten about it. When I noticed the band aid, I took it off and put on a new one. It hurt a little, but by the next day I didn't need a band aid at all. By day three it didn't even hurt anymore. How could that nasty, deep cut heal so quickly, into just a light thin line of loose skin?

This accident reminded me of a spiritual Truth: our physical bodies are divinely created to heal themselves. It is built into our DNA by our loving Mother-Father-Creator God. Surely you have been where I was. You get a nasty paper cut, or you cut yourself shaving, or you trip and scrape your knee. We bleed, it hurts, we clean it and cover it, and voila! The skin grows back together, and we heal. Sometimes we scar, but we always heal.

It's not just our skin. If you ever broke a bone when you were a kid, I bet it is not still broken! Bones heal. My youngest daughter fell off the monkey bars when she was six and broke the humerus bone in her arm. As a parent, it was a good example of knowing on the one hand, her body was designed to heal itself, and on the other hand, she needed to see a doctor ASAP to help facilitate the healing! When we understand that God is everywhere, everyone, and everything, we know that seeking outside help for healing can be a wonderful opportunity to discover God-in-action.

The orthopedic surgeon explained to me that it was one of the worst breaks he had ever seen. (Do they always say that?) Apparently, her bone shattered like eggshells instead of a typical across-the-bone break. I was horrified, and assumed the surgery he had just performed would not help her heal.

The surgeon explained that she would be fine, that if a bone breaks, no matter how badly, the pieces seek each other out and automatically fuse back together. He told me a story about how in medical school he was shown pictures and x-ray films of children in undeveloped third world countries with broken arm and leg injuries that seemed dreadful — yet sure enough, with no access to medical care, no surgery, no setting or casting of the wound, the bones would fuse together, heal, and the child would simply adapt to the new bone formation.

He was right about my daughter. With the combined wisdom of his medical training and the natural tendency of her body to restore itself, her bone healed wonderfully, and all that remained was a small scar from the surgery incision. Bones are designed to heal. Everything in our bodies is designed to heal because God meant for us to experience perfect health, wholeness, and balance in our physical manifestations (our bodies.) Our bones, our organs, our body systems, all the way down to the trillions of tiny cells in our bodies are each designed to function toward wellness, renewal, vitality, and perfect health. The cells in our bodies heal because they cannot help themselves! There is a life force energy that is constantly at work within us. It's spiritual law.

That is a powerful reminder. In our humanness, we tend to forget how intelligent our bodies really are and how powerful we are as spiritual beings. As the developer of chiropractic, B. J. Palmer, said, "The power that made the body, heals the body." I do not necessarily have to understand it scientifically, but I can certainly believe it spiritually, with faith.

In the Bible, James 5:15 tells us, "The prayer of faith will save the sick and the Lord will raise them up." The prayer of faith can simply be a statement of belief in some power which is able, ready, and willing to do the healing. This can translate into a belief in a myriad of things: belief in the human body, belief in a medical doctor, belief in an alternative health practitioner, belief in God's healing power, belief in a prescription, and even belief in a placebo! Any of these beliefs or a combination of beliefs can positively influence the natural order of healing.

Our attitude of thought, our expectations, our consciousness, and most of all our acceptance of the spiritual Truth of healing plays a prominent role in how we experience our good in terms of our health and healing. These ideas lead us to a better understanding of the miracles available to us as children of God. May we replace all our fears with the confident, trusting faith in our perfect health and wholeness. May we remember our divine power, our unlimited potential, and our innate capacity to heal.

The life force energy within us is always good,
and it is always moving in the direction
of balance, harmony, and wholeness.

New Year, New Intentions

INTENTION SETTING

E very year on New Year's Day, something wonderful happens. The calendar year restarts itself, and there is a blank slate before us. A reset for everyone. We have an opportunity to start over and make things new. At the beginning of a new year, it is common to want to look ahead to the future and open ourselves to the endless possibilities before us. We might even want to make changes in our lives, set some goals, or make a *resolution.*

Oh, the dreaded New Year's resolution. We have all made them. We have all broken them. From a spiritual perspective, I am not a huge fan. Resolution comes from the word resolve, and to resolve means to find a solution to a problem. Contrary to what you might believe, you are not a problem! Too often we set a resolution because we are looking backwards and judging ourselves. We are looking at our past behavior over the last year and saying things like: "I didn't exercise enough last year — I need to lose some weight. I eat too much junk food. I think I drink too much wine..." and on and on. So, we set a resolution to exercise and lose weight, to eat better, drink less wine, etc. and then we inevitably break the resolution and feel lousy about ourselves — like a failure. Resolutions might work for some people, but there is always this little negative element of judging ourselves — instead of accepting and loving ourselves.

Alternatively, *intentions* are different. An intention is an act of determining mentally upon some result. Setting an intention is positive and hopeful, a shift in mindset that brings about possibilities. It is a starting point. Our creative power lies in what we intend with the words we speak and the thoughts we think. As divine expressions and children of God, which we all know we are — we have the power within us to create, manifest, claim our good, and make our lives new. These ideas of a new beginning, new life, renewal, rebirth, being born again... this might sound familiar. These are biblical concepts!

There is the notion of renewal in Ephesians: "... be made new in the attitude of your minds; put on the new self, created to be like God," (Eph. 4:23-24). In Romans, Saint Paul reminds us to: "... be transformed by the renewing of your mind — that you may prove what IS, that good and acceptable and perfect will of God," (Rom. 12:2). We are supposed to create this new life WITH God, our Source, using the spiritual principles Christ taught.

I think that is really my problem with New Year's resolutions. Any fool can set a resolution, (myself included) but setting an intention is like co-creating our lives with the will of God in mind. And that is when the magic happens. That is when we can focus on what we DO want to bring into our lives for the coming year, or any time of year. Intention setting is not limited to New Year's Day. We can set an intention on any day we choose. Birthdays are great turning points in the calendar and good opportunities for intention setting. *Any* day is a new day for a new beginning!

Intentions are most powerful when they are written down. I write mine in a journal first and then also sometimes on a little note that I can tuck away somewhere safe, like in my wallet or in my purse — or, as I refer to it "the great spiritual abyss." I've been known to keep intentions under my pillow or taped to the bathroom mirror. I once attended a Unity church where they had us write our New

Year's intention as a letter to ourselves. They collected them and mailed them to us in June, halfway through the year. It isn't so much about where we put the intention or what we do with it, but obviously, what it says. Unsure what to write? Consider these two main questions if you're stuck:

- How do you want to feel in the coming year?
- What is the good you want to draw to you and bring into your life?

Think about the Law of Attraction and vibrational energy. Maybe you want to bring in the energy of love, happiness, abundance, wellness, creativity, or security. It can be something you already have — and you're grateful for, but you want more of it! It is amazing how little we think about what we actually want in life, our highest good, our deepest desires. Take some time to dream up your best life, the one God wants for you!

Setting an intention is not much different than praying. It is co-creating with God. There is great power in clarifying, writing down, and declaring our intentions. Be bold. Seek the Truth of what you want for your life. What do you want to be true for you this year? Ask for it, and intend it. Matthew 7:7 reminds us:

"Ask and it will be given to you,
seek and you will find,
knock and the door will be opened unto you."

We Are One

UNITY WITH ALL LIFE

W e see it everywhere we look. It is on television, radio, newspapers, social media, and the internet in general. It is on bumper stickers, t-shirts, billboards, and signs people carry in the streets (you know, when they are angry and marching against the latest thing that has them outraged.) It is in videos that go viral, and it is in the tone of people's voices when they think no one is listening.

I am talking about all the ways in which we are divided. Our world and our nation struggle with political divisiveness, racial hostility and discrimination, gender inequality, a growing dichotomy between the rich and poor, LGBTQ+ injustice, religious intolerance, and many more polarizing issues. It seems we believe in our separateness more and more every day. But our belief in our separateness is just that... a belief. We know beliefs can be false. They can also be acknowledged, released, and (this is the hard part...) CHANGED. The challenge, I think, is that the ways in which we are united we often can't see.

Perhaps you've seen the meme with several skeletons called 'We're All the Same.' Under each skeleton is a description: White, Black,

Gay, Straight, Religious, Atheist... and then the last one says Pirate. That skeleton is missing a leg bone — get it? Har har! It's a funny joke, but it demonstrates for us that deep down at our core, in our bones, we really are all the same. We really are one. (Okay, except for those pesky Pirates.) But there is something bigger connecting us than just bones on the inside. It is the truth of who and what we are — the truth of our spiritual oneness — and it is not a new concept.

Carl Sagan suggested years ago that the very matter that makes up all of us was originally generated in the stars, that, in a sense, humans are children of the stars. That means we are naturally interconnected because the components of our bodies are not only ancient, but the same. We are one. A similar message appears in a quote frequently attributed to Pierre Teilhard de Chardin: "We are not human beings having a spiritual experience. We are spiritual beings have a human experience." When we harmonize with this idea that we are all spiritual beings, coming from Spirit, consisting of Spirit, expressing as Spirit, a true state of peace comes over us.

The same wisdom and intelligence that exists within you, exists within all human beings. Too often we allow ourselves to be distracted and influenced by our patriotic, religious, "group" interests. Humanity is like one expansive body, and each one of us is a cell in this body. The spiritual truth of our oneness must supersede our ego's attachment to being Democrat, Republican, black, white, American, gay, straight, Christian, Muslim, rich, poor, male, female, etc. We are all a part of the same humanity simply because we are alive. All life is one in Spirit, as Spirit.

The Christian Bible teaches: "Make every effort to keep the unity of the Spirit through the bond of peace. There is one body and one Spirit, just as you were called to one hope when you were called; one Lord, one faith, one baptism; one God and Father of all, who is over all and through all and in all" (Eph. 4:3-6).

Ernest Holmes writes in *The Science of Mind*®, "It would be impossible to make a clearer statement of Truth: One Life behind all that lives! One, One, One... never two. The unity of all life. To learn this is to know a secret of the ages."[1] The unity of all life truly is a secret of the ages, and it is one we can make a conscious effort to know, remember, and trust.

Our true power lies in our oneness.
Let's change the world together.

Affirmative Prayer: The Great Experiment

AFFIRMATIVE PRAYER/SPIRITUAL MIND TREATMENT

When I was young, I often sought spiritual help from a state of desperation, praying a prayer of supplication, begging and beseeching a God-power that I thought was outside of me. I used prayer as an opportunity to bring my wants, desires, and needs to God in the form of a sad laundry list of complaints, mostly regarding my sickness, loneliness, or lack. I prayed like that for a long time, until it started to not make sense anymore.

I eventually learned that praying from a place of want, a sense of need, or a feeling of lack, doesn't get good results. I came to understand that the reason it doesn't work is because God does not know what any of those things are. How could God understand want, need, or lack, when God is unlimited abundance and infinite Good? How can we expect God to answer our prayers when we aren't even speaking the same language?

Praying from a place of need (whether it be for money, material things, healing, love, opportunity, etc.) doesn't work because — just maybe — we don't actually *have* needs. I am aware how cuckoo this sounds. Like you, I don't have to go further than my own community to see humans in need. But if our faith is strong, we know it is our Father's good pleasure to give us the kingdom (Luke 12:32). God is not aware of any need; our needs are always met IF… we choose to believe that. Our belief is always the key!

When we have a desire, whatever the desire may be, the thing we desire exists already — somewhere, somehow, in some form — otherwise how could we even desire it? Invisible desires exist, even if only in imagination. Whether it be a material thing, wealth, health, joy, etc. that we desire, it is not truly absent from us if we believe that God is never absent from us. How could God be absent if we believe God is All? Whatever and whoever exists, exists in and as God. There can be no separateness. This is what Jesus spoke of when he affirmed: "I and the Father are One" (John 10:30). Jesus was not the great exception; he was our great example — the master teacher who understood his unity with the Infinite Intelligence of God and demonstrated our true human potential.

The Power of God's Spirit is everywhere, like an infinite field of energy, and we are in the Presence of this God-Power all the time. We are one with it. Recognizing this Presence is the key to our prayers being as powerful and effective as possible. Focusing our attention on this truth is what grants us access to the Power. This is why the Bible tells us, "Seek the kingdom of God, and all these things shall be added to you" (Luke 12:31).

If we believe that God is our Good, ever present in all forms, visible and invisible, then of what could we ever really want or need? To pray from a place of need is to misunderstand God and God's spiritual law. Our Good (which is synonymous with God) is all around us, waiting for it to be realized. True prayer is declaring and realizing the truth that everything in our being is God. Our focus must be on God, first, the Source of All, and our oneness with It. We must speak in the language of God's Truth, from the place of our indwelling Divinity, so there is no confusion. No matter what the world of appearances might look like, no matter what the condition is that sparks and motivates us to pray, we must not be disturbed by it. It is our job to be firmly rooted in our unity with Spirit and affirm our Godly truth — our peace, love, joy, abundance, health, and well-being.

This is why affirmative prayer (also known as spiritual mind treatment) is so powerful. It uses this creative process as a spiritual tool to navigate life. It involves thinking and believing things already are as you would prefer them to be, until whatever perfect God quality you have pictured in your mind has manifested into existence and into your experience. While the methods of affirmative prayer can vary slightly in different churches, the idea is the same, following these main steps:

- Recognizing the omnipresent Spirit of God
- Acknowledging unity with the Presence of God
- Declaring the Divine Truth of the experience (regardless of whether it is visible or not)
- Giving thanks for it all
- Releasing the prayer

This type of prayer is methodical and precise. It is testable. Everyone can analyze through their own consciousness whether they are achieving the outcomes they wish to see. Students of New Thought recognize that prayer is the habit and art of right thinking, of becoming so conscious of the Presence of God within us that we naturally draw to us all the things that are fundamental for a good, abundant life. It is from this place of knowing that we use affirmative prayer as a declaration of truth. Affirmative prayer does not have to be flowery or overly complicated. For instance, my go-to affirmative prayer for health and well-being goes like this:

- *I recognize that God is all there is, and God is only Good.*
- *I understand that I am one with God. My ever-present Good surrounds me.*

- *Whatever the outcome and truth I wish to experience, I claim it as my good right here and now. I am healthy and happy! All is well.*
- *I am grateful for all the ways God's truth unfolds in my experience.*
- *Releasing this prayer, I let it go, trusting and expecting its fulfillment. And So It Is.*

I believe the objective of affirmative prayer is to be so focused on the Presence of God, so unified with Spirit and therefore aligned with our truth, that we cannot help but manifest our highest good and best life experience. It will naturally unfold and be revealed, with no effort on our part because that's the way spiritual Law works. As Jesus taught, it is the Father (the Power) within that does the work.

Our experience is the outcome of our inner vision, what we believe and affirm. Test affirmative prayer for yourself and see!

Peace: The Case for a Breathing Space

SEEKING PEACE, STILLNESS/SILENCE

I am friends with a CSL minister who has struggled with addiction, various health issues, and financial difficulties for many years. His faith is strong, and his use of spiritual principle is even stronger. He has persevered and thrived over the years I have known him, creating many positive changes in his conditions. When I asked him his secret for overcoming so much, he admitted that he has really only prayed and treated consistently for one thing in his life: peace. He believed if he could manifest that, everything else would fall into place. He did, and it has. His story intrigued me and reminded me of Paul's message to the Philippians: *"Do not be anxious about anything, but in every situation, by prayer and petition, with thanksgiving, present your requests to God. And the peace of God, which transcends all understanding, will guard your hearts and your minds in Christ Jesus"* (Phil. 4:6-7).

How we could all benefit from experiencing the peace that passes all understanding! Think about how positively the entire world would benefit if everyone was actively seeking and trusting in the truth of God's peace. My friend made many life changes by focusing on his individual spiritual practice, which makes sense. Peace is found within us. As much as we like to tell ourselves otherwise, deep down we know we need to be looking inward, not outward at the behavior of others, which — let's be honest — is so much easier to do!

When we think of world peace and the obstacles to it, it always seems to be about the "other guy's behavior." Remember, when you point one finger out, (and probably give it a good wagging) there are always three other fingers pointing back at you. As the famous hymn states: Let there be peace on earth, and let it begin with me. It does not say: Let there be peace on earth and let it start with all those annoying people who are causing all the problems in the world.

So, if peace begins with each one of us, then that means, (as my friend made clear) we each have spiritual work to do. Humanity is made up of individuals. If we collectively wish to experience peace, it makes sense to start with the individual. We must each become peaceful in our own thoughts to bring about this worldwide change.

A similar idea is found in the prayer for peace that is attributed to Lao Tsu, who wrote the Tao te Ching. It says:

If there is to be peace in the world,
there must be peace in the nations.
If there is to be peace in the nations,
there must be peace in the cities.
If there is to be peace in the cities,
there must be peace between neighbors.
If there is to be peace among neighbors,
there must be peace in the home.
If there is to be peace in the home,
there must be peace in the heart.

This is a lovely sentiment, but it still leaves me wanting more guidance. I'm impatient. I want literal, tangible, advice for how to do this. Peace is an abstract concept. How do you become peaceful? How do you put peace in your heart? My friend used prayer and spiritual mind treatment. Excellent tools, but could it be even simpler? Can putting peace in our heart be as simple as taking the time to be still and realize that it is already there?

Some New Thought spiritual centers have what is called a "Silence Room," in which no speech or discussion is to take place. Used only for stillness, silent prayer, and meditation, the room is designed to cultivate and recognize peace within the heart. It is a wonderful idea, but how often do we visit our spiritual centers to utilize such a room?

When we consider how much more time we spend in our homes, it may behoove us to dedicate a silent space in our living environment to cultivate peace in our hearts there. Think about it: we have a kitchen in our house for cooking our food, a dining room for eating, a living room for watching television, a bedroom for sleeping, but where do we go when we just want to be alone, be still, and be quiet? Where can we practice becoming aware of the peace within us? What if we consciously set up such a space? Since most of us don't have an entire spare room to designate for this, we could choose to create just a space in our house, perhaps in the corner of a room that could be beneficial to the whole family. This isn't much different than the "time out corner" parenting method designed to quiet and calm down toddler behavior, except all ages can utilize this peaceful space.

Every time we felt agitated or troubled, we could go to that space, sit down in silence, breathe, and think about the peace that exists inside us. We might call this peacefully focusing on the breath of God, or mindfully taking the time to be breathed by God. Either way, simple practices like conscious breathing and stillness are essential for our desire for inner peace. Inner peace leads to outer peace. I encourage you to take the time to breathe. Take the time to be still and know. Experience the peace happening in your designated breathing space daily.

Notice the peace happening within your own heart.
It is your goodness unfolding.

A Deserted Place

MEDITATION, STILLNESS/SILENCE

D id you have a bad day? Stressed at work? Are the kids and the spouse driving you crazy? Is the world expecting you to work miracles and you are feeling worn out? I think Jesus felt like that sometimes, too. (Okay, not about the kids and spouse.) He had a great way of dealing with stress though: he found a deserted place. I mean, he did this a LOT.

In Matthew 4, Jesus went to the desert alone, so he could fast and pray and prepare for the temptations he would experience. In Luke 6:12, Jesus departed to the mountain to pray, spending the night in prayer to God. In Mark 1:35, Jesus got up early in the morning, when it was still dark, and went out to a deserted place and prayed. I could go on and on. The bible is nothing if not repetitious, and there is a reason. Any good teacher knows repetition is the key to getting students to remember something important. So, if we are seeing this again and again — Jesus going off to be alone in a deserted place — it must be important.

There is an interesting pattern in the repetitions. The book of Matthew tells us Jesus goes to a solitary place to pray after learning of John the Baptist's murder. Immediately afterwards, he performs the miracle of manifesting the loaves and fishes — where he feeds the 5,000. And then, the scene ends with Jesus going back up on the mountain by himself, to pray. The same miracle appears in the Gospel of Mark, and there, it says, "After bidding them farewell, he left for the mountain to pray" (Mark 6:46). When he comes back down from the mountain in that version, he walks on water for his disciples and proceeds to heal a multitude of people who have lined the streets.

The pattern is: pray in a solitary place, manifest a miracle, pray in a deserted place, come back and perform healing miracles, and so on. There are more examples of miracles being sandwiched between solitary time alone to pray. In Luke, great multitudes come to Jesus to be healed, and the next line says, "Jesus, withdrew himself into the wilderness and prayed" (Luke 5:16). Later in Luke, chapter 6, Jesus went to a mountain to pray, and continued all night in prayer to God (Luke 6:12). Guess what he does when he comes down? He heals a great multitude of people (Luke 6:18-19).

This is definitely a pattern of behavior. I always say Jesus is our great teacher and our great example for how to live our lives on earth and claim our good. Jesus is demonstrating self-care and spiritual practice. He is instructing us how to take time to rest, be still, and most importantly, how to have a relationship with our creator God, the Universe, our Divine Source. Taking the time to do this might be as necessary to humans as getting enough food and sleep.

So, what do self-care and spiritual practice look like? Maybe you wonder, like me — what exactly was Jesus doing in these deserted places? I think he was praying, meditating, seeking connection with the Divine, being still, being open and receptive, focused on being ready to receive inspiration. How do I know he was ready to receive inspiration? Because Jesus was frequently inspired. The man had great ideas and executed some pretty amazing miracles using the power of God within him. Maybe you need inspiration, too. Maybe you need to connect with your own God-like power. Look to the behavior of Jesus. Think self-care, spiritual practice, silence, and stillness.

Einstein told us, "I think 99 times and find nothing. I stop thinking, swim in silence, and the Truth comes to me." The best part is, the places we go, the type of silent stillness we practice — whether it be prayer, meditation, contemplation, whatever — that can be different for each one of us. You do not have to go spend forty days in the wilderness. A deserted place can be any room in your house. For me, it's a bathtub at 6:30 am before anyone in the house is awake. I have had many a fantastic prayer session in there, reading spiritual texts and meditating in the silence. It is our intention to seek time with God that matters.

Connection with the divine can look and feel like so many different things: feeling the presence of a spirit guide, sensing an angel near, receiving a divine download, having an imagined conversation with Jesus, or simply resting in the stillness within your own heart. Consciously choosing to surrender is the key. It brings clarity, wisdom, and peace when we circle back to our humanness.

When we separate ourselves from others, seeking that daily union, going within the stillness — I promise you, our lives are better for it. If you are needing encouragement, permission, or a gentle nudge, go ahead and do it. Take the bubble bath, go for a walk, indulge in a nap.

Find your deserted place to be alone and surrender.
You deserve it.

Have it More Abundantly

PROSPERITY/ABUNDANCE AS SPIRITUAL PRINCIPLE

When most people hear the word abundance, they think of wealth or affluence — having plenty of money or financial resources. While it certainly can mean that, it can also mean an extremely plentiful or over-sufficient supply of anything, not just things having to do with money. Abundance exists automatically in nature. Have you ever seen a giant tree that chooses not to fill itself with leaves on every branch? Of course not, it just grows abundantly without even trying! Would an animal living in the wild choose not to enjoy the food and water that it came upon? Of course not, it would eat and drink happily, enjoying what nature so abundantly provides.

We humans are part of nature, too. Abundance is our natural birthright. It is how God intends for us to live — abundantly! Remember the Good Shepherd illustration Jesus gave? "I have come that they may have life, and that they may have it more abundantly" (John 10:10). Knowing that abundance can mean "many" of all sorts of good things, like harmonious relationships, business and career opportunities, fresh food to eat, clean water to drink, a comfortable home to live in, good health, friends and family, unexpected blessings, expressions of kindness, and so on, it is worth paying attention to whether we are really choosing to live abundantly.

And yes, it is a choice. Humans sometimes unintentionally create conditions of lack, scarcity, and poverty for themselves. We have already discussed the spiritual principle that it is done unto us as we believe. When we believe our own limiting thoughts and beliefs, negative conditions and a lack of abundance occur. We carry thoughts and beliefs from yesterday, last month, last year, all the way back into our childhoods. Have you ever stopped to consider why you think and believe what you do about abundance in general?

Unfortunately, many people mistakenly believe there is never enough, or worse, that there might be enough, but not for them. They believe that they don't deserve to live abundantly, for whatever reason. This is simply not the truth; those are false beliefs. Divine abundance is limitless and available to all. It is only our ability to receive that influences our lack or surplus of abundance. It has been said that divine abundance is much like the vastness of an ocean, a limitless supply of water available to all. However much we carry away depends on the size of the container we bring. If we bring a five-gallon bucket, we get five gallons, but if we bring a shot glass, we get only a shot glass full. We are the only ones who limit our ability to receive, not God.

Indeed, this spiritual process is based on our own receptivity. When looking at the amount of abundance you are experiencing and all the blessings (or perceived lack of blessings) in your life, do take the time to consider the size of your vessel. Divine abundance is your birthright. Claim it as so, by being open and receptive to all the good our God-Source wants to bestow on you.

How much good can you receive?
Only as much as you believe!

Best Valentine's Day Ever

LOVING OTHERS

Question: Of all the Valentine's Days you have experienced in your life, what was the best one? Mine was back in the early 1980's. I was probably eight or nine years old. My dad came home from work and said, "I got you a Valentine's Day present. I hid it in the living room. I bet you'll never find it!" I don't think I understood sarcasm yet.

This was fun. A game! A gift! I ran to the living room. I was hoping for a new stuffed animal with a heart on it — I loved stuffed animals! But I figured it was probably candy, for sure. Boy, was I wrong. Propped up against the wall behind one of our living room chairs was a brand-new red plastic sled. Huh? I was so confused. I didn't know a sled could be a Valentine's Day gift. It turns out, yes, it can.

Don't get me wrong, I was really happy! My old sled had recently gotten a crack in it that was making it more and more difficult to use. My dad gave me something I truly loved — and something I couldn't wait to use! He was expressing love for me, his child, by a) fixing my broken sled problem, and b) gifting me something that would bring me joy. It was the first time I realized a Valentine's Day gift could be about parental love.

Love between parent and child is just one of four types of love. From the ancient Greek, it is called Storge, and it means familial love. It refers to a natural instinctual affection, such as the love a parent feels toward their children. Usually, the kind of love we see marketed for Valentine's Day is Eros — romantic love — including desirous feelings and physical attraction. Philia refers to affectionate love between friends, characterized by loyalty and trust. It is platonic, yet meaningful and sweet. The increasingly popular "Galentine" celebrations, where women gather to love and empower each other on or around February 13th, are a great example of this kind of love.

Agape is universal love. It is selfless love of man for God and of God for man. It can also include love for strangers, those less fortunate, and all mankind. Spiritual in nature, agape love is often considered sacrificial and even radical. It is the core message of Jesus' teaching. He told us that the two most important commandments are to love God with all our soul and to love our neighbor as ourselves (Mark 12:29-31). I think the best way to do this is by making a conscious effort to keep our awareness on love.

That is why I like using Valentine's Day as an example. We are all consciously aware of love on that day, whether we want to be or not! We might see men carrying flower bouquets, children eating heart shaped candies, couples going out to dinner, and people buying bakery treats, cards, and helium balloons. There is a sense of joy and a lightness of spirit that many people feel on Valentine's Day. Spiritually, it goes much deeper than that.

Love is a state of being. It is what I am, and it is what you are. Figuratively speaking, love is a noun before it can be a verb. When first we recognize that we are made up of divine love — and we are surrounded by this love — we can then choose to live, move, and have our being in it, expressing it outward to others. Whether it is parental, romantic, platonic, or universal, we always have the opportunity to express love. The red hearts that pop up all over the place every February remind me of this. Valentine's Day makes me nostalgic for all the simple, sometimes silly ways we can show love for others. The expression of our love does not have to be expensive, heavy, or intense, nor does it have to be limited to one day of the year.

It needs to be acknowledged that not everyone loves Valentine's Day. It hurts when we feel lonely and think that no one loves us (which is a false thought.) When we mistakenly believe we are lacking love in our lives, choosing to shift our awareness to the divine love within us is crucial. As we then make the choice to outwardly express love for others, it draws to us the very thing we think we are missing. When we give love freely, love returns to us. If you think I'm wrong, why not try it and see? Call a friend, engage with an acquaintance, visit a neighbor. "Love your neighbor" just means "Love your ANYONE."

Love is something to consciously put into practice; it is constantly in motion, flowing, and in circulation. It is a lot easier to receive what we are already freely giving. Being consciously aware of the divine love within us as we outwardly love others is an opportunity to reveal and reclaim our own good — more love in our own lives!

Who can you love today? How can you love today?

The Wagon Wheel Lesson

INTERFAITH/HONORING ALL PATHS TO GOD

"There are hundreds of paths up the mountain, all leading to the same place, so it doesn't matter which path you take. The only person wasting time is the one who runs around the mountain, telling everyone that his or her path is wrong."

Hindu Proverb

Whenever I tell someone that I am an Interfaith Minister, I usually get a blank stare back — sometimes with a polite nod — and sometimes with an immediate follow up question: "What does that mean?"

Interfaith Ministry is a broad umbrella term referring to cooperation and positive interaction between different religions. It requires education and study. It is important work. Speaking in the most general terms, my colleagues and I:

- encourage harmony between religions and people
- create opportunities for safe dialogue

- explore various concepts that different faith traditions have in common
- promote unity
- (especially in my case) contemplate the idea of a universal God.

Each person on earth can and should follow a unique spiritual path deserving of validation, reverence, and respect. My role is that of a bridge builder and communicator. I support and help an individual's spiritual journey so that it is aligned with their soul purpose. I believe in the unity of all life, and as I say repeatedly: I honor all paths to God.

Some of the most unfortunate acts that can arise from people not honoring other paths to God are mass shooting tragedies that involve someone storming into a place of worship and murdering people who are peacefully practicing their chosen religion. When I hear about these senseless tragedies, I am emboldened to work even harder.

There is no reason to judge others for being on a different spiritual path. (I applaud people for being on any path at all these days!) I celebrate anyone who has the spiritual wherewithal and desire to seek and connect with our Divine Source in whatever way they want. Projecting our beliefs on others has never made any sense to me. Just as I told my students when I taught second grade, it also fits to tell the grown-ups of the world: "Just worry about yourself!"

One of the most meaningful and fortunate things I have been asked to do is talk to church youth groups, confirmation classes, or high school students about Interfaith Ministry. The workshop style lesson I present to them is called, "The Wagon Wheel."

The lesson goes like this...

Picture a giant wagon wheel like the one in the illustration. Sometimes I draw one out on the white board, or display one in a PowerPoint, or we all draw it on paper in front of us. In the center of the wagon wheel is GOD. I use the word God, but as we know, some people don't like that word. You can put a different word in the center if you prefer, like Allah, Father, Jehovah, Yahweh, Holy Spirit, Creator, Source, the Universe etc. You know the drill: use the word that works for you.

From the center of the wagon wheel there are spokes that come out and connect to the larger, circular "tire" part of the wheel. On each spoke of the wagon wheel is an individual religion or a faith tradition that a person could practice. Some examples are Christianity (which would include all the different denominations of that religion) Judaism, Hinduism, Islam, Sikhism, Jainism, African religions, Chinese traditional religions, Primal-Indigenous traditions, Bahai, Buddhism, etc. With over 4,000 religions in the world, there are a LOT of possible spokes.

I explain to the kids that people practice their chosen religion, and that religion brings them closer to... (follow the spoke to the center)... you guessed it, God! We can get closer to God by following any of the spokes on the wheel, and it doesn't matter which one we are on. We end up in the same central spot: God. We are all human, and we are all different. The idea is to find the spoke (faith tradition) that works for each of us as individuals.

In my lesson, I often label one of the spokes Atheism. Is Atheism really a religion? A quick google search of that question shows exhaustive arguments on both sides, and the truth is, I don't care whether it is factually considered a religion or not. Atheists are human beings. Their choice to not practice an organized religion, to me, is a "practice." Consider this: Plenty of adult children choose to have nothing to do with their parents and stay estranged from them. They are still technically the children of those parents. I consider atheists to be children of God. They might not believe that, but I do, and I believe God does. So, they get a spoke on the wheel in my lesson. I can still validate and respect their spiritual path (or non-spiritual path.)

When I hear about the people who commit acts of violence and terror against a faith community, I often wonder, who was around them before they made their deadly decision? Who listened to them? Did they talk to family members, or friends, or coworkers? Were they posting online about their plans? Who agreed with their anger and their ideas? Were they encouraged? Who sat by silently and neglected to point out their skewed logic and unacceptable thinking? Did anyone at all in their lives miss the opportunity to show respect for all paths to God and demonstrate open mindedness?

This is what I tell young students I teach. Each of us can be a person who builds bridges and potentially stops tragedies. If you hear someone badmouthing another faith tradition, speak up and say something. Be brave. Lead by example. Go out of your way to accept others. When you do not understand something about another religion, ask! Education helps us all. Learn about how others go about their spiritual practice, what rituals they perform, and the ways they love God. Chances are you will find you have more things in common than not.

Nothing bad happens when
we learn about someone else's religion.
On the contrary, something good happens!
We make the oneness of humanity even stronger.
This is a natural demonstration of our good.

Mirror, Mirror, Spiritual Practice

LOVING THE SELF

Innumerable spiritual strategies and practices exist out there. Not all of them will resonate. I know I have tried many, and I still end up clinging stubbornly to my favorites. We do the things that work for us, the things that bring us closer in our relationship with God, Spirit, Universe, Source.

I would like to take this opportunity to discuss my least favorite spiritual practice. Yes, you read that right. My least favorite spiritual practice is... self-love. I can hear you now, "Self-love is a spiritual practice?" Yes, it is! It's not my least favorite to talk about or teach, but it is literally my least favorite to use in my own life. Why? Because it is hard work, and it is deeply personal. The good news is this practice has great impact on our lives.

We are all familiar with that important commandment: Love your neighbor as yourself. When we hear it, we tend to gloss over the last two words. If we do anything at all, we immediately start focusing on loving our neighbor — reaching out to them, showing compassion, caring about them, forgiving them, etc. We forget that there are two components to the commandment. It doesn't just say,

"Love your neighbor." It says, "Love your neighbor AS YOURSELF."

We are supposed to be loving our neighbors in the same way we love ourselves. What way is that, exactly? We are supposed to be paying attention to, showing compassion for, and caring about *ourselves*. It is weird to think about, isn't it? It seems like that would be a natural inclination, but the truth is, sometimes we don't treat ourselves so lovingly. I am talking about negative self-talk, criticizing myself, thinking I'm not good enough, and generally not loving myself.

Louise Hay spent decades in her groundbreaking career as a speaker, author, and publisher teaching people to love themselves. Her bestselling book, *You Can Heal Your Life*, offers a life-changing look at the way we think about, talk about, and treat ourselves. (I would go so far as to call it required reading for anyone on a New Thought, spiritually mindful path toward healing, living their best life, and revealing their highest good.) If we believe in the idea of a Creator God, who creates life, who *is* life, then we are, each of us, a child of God, born perfect, whole, and complete. I invite you to think about that and consider what that means to you. We are all magnificent, divine beings.

It makes sense that we should be loving ourselves the way the living Spirit of God loves us. God would never call you stupid, or think you are unworthy, or judge you for mistakes you have made. The God presence within you is your biggest cheerleader in life. Use your own mind, your own thoughts to tap into God's acceptance, approval, and love. It is within you, and it is powerful. Speak kindly to yourself; forgive yourself. Make a conscious effort to love and approve of yourself.

In fact, Louise Hay recommended saying loving statements to yourself while looking in the mirror[1]. Go on, give it a try. Look at yourself in the mirror right now, and say out loud: "(your name,) I love you. I love and approve of who you are. I accept you for who you are." Affirm for yourself: "I am a child of God, perfect, whole, and complete. I am loved."

Don't be surprised if it feels weird, silly, or even emotional! Keep practicing. Set a goal to try it every time you happen to pass a mirror. It is a powerful exercise that demonstrates the great love God has for you, to connect and unite your perfect, balanced self.

Love yourself, empower yourself.
Life (capital L-Life) loves you!

Is It Good or Bad?

SEEKING PEACE

S tories are an important part of teaching and learning. That is why the Bible is full of parables, (or as I call them, "the Jesus Riddles"). Whether it be a Christian parable, a Buddhist Koan, a Taoist story, or a personal anecdote from a minister's life, a good classic story can often best illustrate a spiritual lesson.

One of my favorite examples is a Zen story called "Maybe." It cleverly teaches us about aligning ourselves with Life and cautions against labeling life events as good or bad. It goes like this:

A Taoist story tells of an old farmer who had worked his crops for many years. One day his horse ran away. Upon hearing the news, his neighbors came to visit. "Such bad luck," they said sympathetically. "Maybe," the farmer replied. The next morning the horse returned, bringing with it three other wild horses. "How wonderful!" the neighbors exclaimed. "Maybe," replied the old man. The following day, his son tried to ride one of the untamed horses, was thrown, and broke his leg. The neighbors again came to offer their sympathy on his misfortune: "How unfortunate," they said. "Maybe," answered the farmer. The day after, military officials came to the village to draft young men into the army. Seeing that the son's leg was broken, they passed him by. The neighbors congratulated the farmer on how well things had turned out. "Maybe," said the farmer.

You see how the farmer refused to judge the events and circumstances that happened in his life. He simply accepted them for what they were. When we live in alignment with spiritual wisdom, we understand that we can't possibly know how a random event will play out in the big picture of life. This is good advice for us, to neither become thrilled with excitement at seemingly good luck, nor sink into despair over what seems like bad misfortune.

But how hard it is for us to remember this! We are human, after all, and our egos love to label everything. We have emotions and love to react to outside circumstances happening to us. There is a certain level of peacefulness that comes with behaving the way the farmer did, a sense of alignment with the Universe. Choosing not to label situations as good or bad means we aren't resisting reality. We are letting things be and choosing peace. Even William Shakespeare pointed out in Hamlet, "... there is nothing either good or bad, but thinking makes it so."

We need not be imprisoned by our interpretations and thoughts about our circumstances. Students of mindfulness may call this practice simply observing our thoughts, letting the calmness of reality be the focus. From a spiritual perspective, the idea is to allow, embrace, and accept the true stability of God, Spirit, Universe, which as we know, always has our back. This is not easy and can take a lot of conscious effort. After all, we humans love our attachments. We attach ourselves to all kinds of things, like outcomes, people, and material possessions. Don't get me wrong, loss of any of those things is still is a loss. But by choosing not to label a loss as bad and choosing to simply let it be, we are free to live in peace, ready for whatever Life brings us next.

My father understood this well, though it makes me laugh to describe him as "enlightened." (He would laugh at that, too.) He just loved to tell a good story, and the funnier the better. I'm grateful for the many hilarious nuggets of wisdom he gave me before he made his physical transition. One of his favorite stories based on his real-life experience was about how a free car once cost him $20,000.

My father worked hard his entire life, and he had always wanted to own a Cadillac. So, he worked, saved, and eventually, in his mid 60's he was able to buy the least expensive, lowest-end model Cadillac they made. He was so happy! But then, within a few months, things started going wrong with it. First, it was the transmission, then the automatic windows wouldn't work, then there was a glitch in the engine that had to be repaired, then it was the transmission again. It seemed like every other month the car was in the shop, and he was inconvenienced. He wasn't necessarily unhappy, but he was pretty disappointed with his dream car. Then, out of the blue, the dealership called him up and said, "Sir, your car has been in for repairs so many times, General Motors agrees it qualifies for the Lemon Law. You can come down to the dealership and choose any car on the lot. We'd like to replace your car for free." My father was ecstatic! He chose a very beautiful higher-end model, leather everything, GPS, the whole nine yards. He really enjoyed that new car! And then, a couple years later, my dad's wife wanted to divorce him. It was an amicable split, and they went to the attorney together. It was explained to him that under state law, all assets must be split equally according to their value. So, he had to pay his ex-wife over $20,000 in order just to keep driving the FREE car General Motors had gifted him.

Fortunately, my father found this hilarious. He harbored no real anger or resentment over the situation. I remember saying to him, "Wow, doesn't that make you mad?" And he just shrugged and said, "Eh, it's only money," demonstrating his peaceful non-attachment to material things and wealth. Ironically, it would have done him no good to get upset and resist whatever happened because he died of cancer the following year. In the long run, that money was of no use to him anyway! We just never know what kind of plan Spirit has in store for us.

So whether our horse runs off, our child breaks a leg, our car breaks down, or we are hit with an unexpected financial setback, our reaction (or lack of one) is always up to us. Trust the higher order of Spirit. When new horses unexpectedly show up, or our child is spared hardship, or we finally buy our dream car, or we are gifted a free dream car... trust the higher order of Spirit. Choose peace.

Whatever it is, perhaps it isn't good or bad.
Perhaps it simply is.

What Moms Really Want

LOVING OTHERS

Mother's Day always seems like an appropriate time to consider the maternal, nurturing, protective aspects of the Divine. God, being all, of course includes qualities that are masculine, feminine, and everything in between and outside of those labels. *ALL*. God's feminine characteristics are undeniably real.

A little girl once asked her parents, "If God is our father, then who is our mother?" Before they could answer, she said, "Oh, I know! It must be Mother Nature!" That is adorable; yet, it also makes sense, that those elements of nature: beauty, power, harmony, and creativity exist for us to experience our own nurturing and growth. The maternal characteristics of God have great value, and they are worth honoring in the same way we honor our earthly mothers on Mother's Day.

So, how do we usually honor mothers? There is the commercial aspect of course: flowers, jewelry, taking her out to brunch, etc. But what do moms really want? I have three grown daughters who no longer live at home, but every year when they were little, they would ask me what I wanted for Mother's Day. Every year I would tell them the same thing: I want world peace and a clean house. (There was always a chance that they might clean something...).

When they were teenagers, I realized they didn't really understand what I meant by world peace. I wasn't expecting them to single handedly solve all the global international conflicts. What I wanted was peace in MY WORLD. Peace in MY house, Peace in MY family. So, I had to specifically say, "What I want is for you to get along with your sisters all day. No fighting." Of course, what I was asking for, what I wanted, was for them to love each other. This is the same thing Jesus tells us to do. "This is my commandment: Love One Another" (John 15:12). It is the most loving, joyous, positive commandment, and it is also quite parental. In fact, it's very motherly!

When children focus on their mutual love of their mother and put aside their differences and get along — even for just one day — it is very pleasing for the mother. Even when they are faking it. Delight comes in the effort. The best part is it doesn't cost anything! The gift of getting along is a free, relatively simple way to make mom happy. As God's children, what a gift to the Universe, humanity, and one another, to live in harmony, peace, and love!

Everywhere we see divided communities, a divided nation, a divided world, with war, threats of war, displaced refugees, hatred, and suffering. Let us delight in the effort it takes to love people who behave and think differently than we do. Let's find the joy in loving people of other faiths, or even people of no faith. Let's delight in our trying, in our awareness, and in our feeblest of attempts to love one another, for deep down we know that all people are our brothers and sisters, and there really is no "other."

St. Thomas Aquinas wrote in the 13th century:

How is it they live for eons in such harmony
The billions of stars
When most men can barely go a minute
Without declaring war in their mind

against someone they know.
How can we live in harmony? First, we need to know
We are all madly in love with the same God.

While God's characteristics are unlimited, let us pause to honor and give thanks for the way the living Spirit nurtures us, provides our every need, and indeed loves us, like a mother. May we strive to be greater expressions of God's unconditional love. Let us accept the harmonious, loving nature of our Mother God, and the ability to truly love one another.

Living in harmony reveals the peace of God in our lives.

On Meditation

MEDITATION

R eading about meditation is like reading about swimming. It's not a bad idea, necessarily. You might learn some valuable information, but until you suck it up, get in the pool, and get wet (often) you won't get very far. Books and essays about meditation can fall flat because the underlying message is usually:

1. Just do it.
2. Do it regularly.
3. By the way, it's pretty much the best way to recognize your unity with the God-Source.

No pressure or anything! After meditating faithfully for twelve years or so, I have zero suggestions for how to do it successfully because I'm not sure I have ever done it successfully. (Am I selling you on this spiritual practice yet?) I'm not sure I know what successful meditation is, to be honest. Enlightenment? Levitation? Reaching a level of peace that passes all understanding? Transcending to another realm? All of the above? If that is successful meditation, I guess I am a big, fat failure. But I'm a happy, content failure!

What I do know about my meditation practice is this: it absolutely brings me closer to God, and I love it. There are other benefits, too, according to doctors, scientists, psychologists, and other people who are much smarter than I am. I won't bore you with a huge list, but here are a few highlights of the benefits of regular meditation:

Lower blood pressure, decreased heart rate, quicker recovery from stress, synchronization of right and left hemispheres of the brain, muscle relaxation, peace of mind, fewer mood swings, increased empathy, reduced anxiety, deeper connection with others, deeper sense of purpose, potential for transcendental experiences.

I would add: *it just feels good*. Especially if I keep doing it. That does seem to be the key. I have to do it and do it consistently. While I don't have any "do this, not that!" type suggestions, I have learned a few things over the years that have drastically improved my meditation practice. They may help you, and they may not work for you at all. Please take what helps and leave the rest:

The only goal of meditation is to sense, experience, and unite with God Consciousness. I try not to ask anything other than this when I meditate. I try not to think about anything other than God; try being the key word. Other thoughts obviously happen. I try to observe them and let them pass.

Start small. 5 minutes of meditation is meditation! Be careful not to stay small forever though. Personally, my sweet spot is 15 minutes.

Commit to a daily habit. I mean commit to it like it is your job or it is part of your marriage contract. Take it that seriously. The hardest boundary I ever set was on a Saturday morning when I had to inform my husband that I couldn't dash off to the coffee shop with him until after I had meditated. He got over it.

Meditating at the same time every day helps. Meditating first thing in the morning sets the tone for your day, to the point where you notice a difference in how you feel if you skip it or do it later in the day. Meditating more than once a day, even in short increments, also ups your game.

Don't allow yourself to be disturbed during meditation. That means, no family, no phone, tv, etc. I realize this is a luxury not everyone has available to them, but it matters. You may have to get creative. When my kids were little, I got up early to meditate before anyone else in the house was awake.

Longer, deeper breaths help me relax and begin meditation. Counting breaths or trying to maintain a certain style of breathing tends to cause me anxiety, which is counterintuitive. Simply noticing the breath is a great way to help clear thoughts that have occurred.

There is something about silence. Listening to guided meditations can be powerful and beneficial. They serve a purpose, but relying on them exclusively proved ineffective for me. Silence is somehow more powerful. God is in the silence.

There is something about "darkness." Keeping my eyes closed continuously greatly impacted my meditation experience. God is in the darkness behind my closed eyes.

Meditating outside in nature can be a game changer. Listening to crickets, birds, squirrels, wind chimes, trees blowing, etc. is a great way to notice the "capital L" life all around you. It is deeply meaningful to consider that everything you could possibly hear (with your eyes closed) is created by and expressing as God, including you.

Body position does not matter as much as comfort. The idea is to feel so comfortable that you give no thought to your body at all. Whether you are lying down, sitting on a chair or cross-legged on the floor, it does not matter. A zero-gravity chair was another game changer for me because of how comfortable it is.

If meditation is new to you, just start somewhere — wherever you are, in whatever way you are comfortable. Unsure how? You could certainly read a book on meditation. You could take a class, listen to a podcast, or go to a retreat. All those things can be informative and helpful. But you can also just decide to sit, by yourself, in the silence.

In summary, I guess my underlying message about meditation is:

- Just do it.
- Do it regularly.
- By the way, it's pretty much the best (and perhaps only?) way to recognize your unity with the God-Source.

Good Luck!

A consistent meditation practice helps you stay aware
of the presence of God within you.
The more you do this, the more good is revealed.

A Tapestry on Display

LOVING OTHERS

E ach one of us is an individualized center of God consciousness, each born with our own individuality to be celebrated. Ernest Holmes wrote in his Declaration of Principles, "We believe in the individualization of the Spirit in Us, and that all people are individualizations of the One Spirit."[1] *All People...*

Behind our different faces, each of us is expressing as the one presence of God. Holmes also wrote in his book, Creative Ideas, that it is necessary that we are unique individuals. "Unity," he wrote, "does not mean conformity. Unity means that everything draws its strength, its power, and its ability to live from the one Source."[2] Just because we recognize this need to see our differences and celebrate each other as part of the One, as expressions of the divine, doesn't mean it's an easy thing to do. It is as if we have to back up now and then, to see the bigger picture from time to time. To be able to see as God sees.

Years ago, I worked as a second-grade teacher. I didn't last very long as a teacher because those people are superheroes as far as I'm concerned. I am pretty amazing, but unfortunately, I am not super-hero-level. My favorite subject to teach was art. That was because inevitably, if I had a kid who was struggling and perhaps not excelling academically in math or reading, art was often an opportunity for them to show their talent and realize their gifts and shine. As a teacher, that's a beautiful thing to witness and cultivate.

I would present whatever the art lesson was and give the kids the parameters of the assignment. I would include whatever pieces were required for the project, whatever parts should be on everybody's art piece, and then turn them loose to create. The kids would be zeroed in and focused on their own work, but as the teacher, I could walk around and see all the different expressions coming to life, even though the lesson is the same. The best part is after all the paint had dried, or the glue was dried, and everyone was finished, I got to collect all the projects and take them out into the hallway to display them together for all the world to see.

The kids would come in the next day and be blown away. "Mrs. Paulsen, it's beautiful, look at them all!" I could always rock a hallway display. They were seeing all of them together for the first time. They could step back in the hall and see everyone else's amazing expressions of art right alongside their own. Some were alike, and some were different, but when you looked at them all together like that, they were utterly beautiful.

Side note: there is always a kid who cannot follow directions to save his life. God bless him. He used the wrong colors, he used marker instead of paint, or his project is literally put together backwards and upside down. That expression is still part of the whole. Sometimes you make that one the centerpiece of the collage because it is that magnificent — and you must celebrate it! The whole display is a tapestry of unique expressions.

Sound familiar? If this is a metaphor for all the expressions of life that we see, they are all part of the whole. Even the ones we might not want to recognize because they are so different than we are — they might be a different color, or they might be made with different parts that we don't recognize, or they might seem put together backwards. We know that when Spirit creates, It creates out of Itself. That's all it has to work with. So, the whole universe, the stars, the planets, the earth, the trees and plants, you and me, all life... is made out of the One Spirit — no matter how it's being expressed.

Celebrate the unique individuals
who make up the whole of your life!

A Personal Easter

UNITY WITH THE DIVINE

Holy Week is arguably the most emotional week of the year for Christians. It starts with Christ's triumphant entrance into Jerusalem on Palm Sunday, goes through his last meal with his disciples and his betrayal on Maundy or Holy Thursday, his brutal crucifixion and death on Good Friday, and his physical resting in the tomb on Black or Holy Saturday. Which then brings us to Easter Sunday and the empty tomb. Oh, the empty tomb.

What does the empty tomb mean? That is the question the world was left to think about, and we are still left to consider today. We have been told this story our whole lives, and we have read it again and again. Christians celebrate Easter every year. Believing in this story is something we might come to in different ways, from different paths.

One scripture version of the story has Jesus appearing to Mary Magdalene just outside the empty tomb. Mary gets to SEE Jesus. He calls her by name, and it is then that she recognizes him. Maybe this made her belief in his resurrection a little easier. We know that saying: seeing is believing. Most of us do not have the luxury of that experience of seeing Jesus for ourselves, but we can still come to know and believe in our own way.

I wonder though, is it enough to simply say, yes — I believe this story? I think we do ourselves a disservice if we think this is just a story about a man, Jesus, the Nazarene, a preacher and teacher who considered himself to be one with his Heavenly Father, one with God. We must never forget that we are a part of the story, too. Some say Jesus Christ is really the sum of man's great potential. We can and should contemplate deeply what Easter means for us as individuals and our personal relationship with God.

The message of the resurrection of Christ is one of hope, love, new life, empowerment, and most of all possibility. The possibility of all things — the possibility of overcoming all things. Yes, many believe Christ was and is the Son of God, and in resurrecting himself and bringing his body back to life, he was demonstrating his Divinity. Certainly!

But remember, a spark of that divinity also rests each of us, as a child of God. Easter is not just a day when we recall how Jesus rose from the dead, but it is a time to recognize and develop our own innate divinity, to commit to fulfilling our own divine purpose. We must shed this antiquated notion that we are somehow unworthy and separate from our divine creator God and from the story of Christ's resurrection.

Maybe the true message of Easter is for us to consider our part in the story, to consider that we, too, can achieve unity with our highest self and our highest good. We can master our human experience through our own awakening and rise to embody our spiritual consciousness. We can seriously think about and believe in unlimited possibilities for ourselves because that is our truth. Easter is a blessed time of rebirth, renewal, and reawakening for us all. Let the great I Am come alive and arise in you. I invite you to contemplate your possibilities faithfully, reverently, and joyfully!

What is possible for your life?
What is possible for your health?
What is possible for your relationships?
What is possible for your prosperity and abundance?

The Most Powerful Force in the Universe

LOVING OTHERS

Every time I read about another mass shooting in the United States, I ask myself:

Where do we go from here? The answer is: *We already know.* Spiritually, we know where we are to go. We are to go to forgiveness and love, but when the pain is raw and the loss unbearable, nobody wants to hear that kind of talk. Mass shootings destroy innocent lives again and again and again. We are exhausted from all the mourning. Forgiveness? I'm a minister, and I sometimes I can barely utter the word. How do we get to a place of forgiveness? I wish I had an answer to that.

Scripture tells us what we already know: *Therefore, as God's chosen people, holy and dearly loved, clothe yourselves with compassion, kindness, humility, gentleness and patience. Bear with each other and forgive one another if any of you has a grievance against someone. Forgive as the Lord forgave you. And over all these virtues put on love, which binds them all together in perfect unity.* (Col. 3:12-14)

Yes, God, we know this.

And another familiar one: *I give you a new commandment, that you love one another. Just as I have loved you, you also should love one another.* (John 13:34)

Yes, God, we know this.

Don't forget this one: *Owe no one anything, except to love one another; for the one who loves another has fulfilled the law.* (Rom. 13:8)

We are told repeatedly to love one another. The problem is, I believe most people are already doing this on a daily basis! I see people in my community loving one another. I bet you do, too. I see people loving their own families, their friends, their neighbors, and strangers. I see people I know making the effort to love others, even when it's someone they don't like, when it's uncomfortable, when it's someone who believes in something they don't. If I have just described you, all I can suggest is, 1) keep doing it, and 2) do it even more.

The truth is, when multiple massacres are plaguing the nation and there is conflict and fighting with our leaders instead of unified solutions, we must remember that our healing power lies in our capacity to love, as opposed to seeking revenge or retaliation, or choosing to live in a place of anger and fear.

This is biblical principle:

You shall not take vengeance or bear a grudge against any of your people, but you shall love your neighbor as yourself: I am the Lord. (Lev. 19:18)

Need one more?

To conclude: you must all have the same attitude and the same feelings; love one another, and be kind and humble with one another. Do not pay back evil with evil or cursing with cursing; instead, pay back with a blessing, because a blessing is what God promised to give you when he called you. (1 Pet. 3:8-9)

We see and hear so much anger these days, so much finger pointing. We are getting louder and bolder in our anger, even though we know anger and blame divides us. It undermines the truth of our unity and oneness. It also doesn't bring back one single life.

In case I haven't made this clear, I get angry, too. I think it's important for ministers and spiritual leaders everywhere to admit that. We share your anger and frustration. We feel it, too. I have to remind myself several times a day:

While anger is understandable,
love is powerful.

Loving one another, showing compassion, and blessing others are more powerful than negative emotions like fear and anger, and they are actually more powerful than forceful, evil acts like revenge or murder. It doesn't seem like that would be true, but it is. The weakness or strength of human consciousness — our inherent spiritual nature — can be demonstrated in something called applied kinesiology, also known as muscle testing.

Studies show that muscles will strengthen or weaken in the presence of positive or negative stimuli. The stimuli can be intellectual (something the subject is just thinking about) or physical (something the subject is holding or touching.) If you have never seen a muscle testing demonstration, the best way to explain it is to imagine that I'm standing with one arm stretched straight out in front of me at shoulder level, with my palm facing down. The "tester" tells me she's going to push on my arm, and my job is to resist her pushing and not let my arm go down. Simple enough.

So, she might say, "Think of Jesus Christ," and she tries to push my arm down, but my arm muscles will strengthen and resist solidly. It is easy for me to resist her pushing. If she then says, "Think of Adolph Hitler," and pushes on my arm, it doesn't matter how hard I try to resist, my arm will go weak and go down. This really happens. If you ever get the opportunity to see a presentation on applied kinesiology or muscle testing, go to it — and volunteer because it will blow your mind! It seems like a parlor trick from the 1950's, but so much clinical research has been done on this, and the results are amazingly universal.

Essentially, the more powerful a stimulus, the stronger the muscle test result, as in the positive, loving example of Jesus. The most powerful stimuli are often "God words," like God, Jesus Christ, Love, Compassion, Joy, Peace. I personally feel that the most powerful stimulus is LOVE.

The more forceful a stimulus, the weaker the muscle test result, as in the much-hated, negative example of Hitler. As expected, some of the most forceful stimuli are hateful people, groups, and events that cause intentional loss of human life, such as the Holocaust, the 9/11 attacks, and the violent mass shootings that keep taking place. I believe HATE represents the most forceful stimuli.

The force of hate weakens us and literally makes our muscles test weak. The power of love strengthens us, literally making our muscles test strong. Love is empowering. Is this not the essence of the teachings of Jesus? Our true power lies in our capacity to love. It is up to us to wake up every day and consciously choose to be an expression of love. Even when we are angry and outraged. Even when it is hard. We must make our decisions today based not on our fears, but on our hope of a peaceful, loving world.

Remember that Albert Einstein told us the most important decision we have to make is whether we believe we live in a friendly or hostile universe. What a challenge it is to see friendliness, love, compassion, and our oneness, when hostility and hatred are so prevalent. My prayer is that we faithfully make that choice to move forward in hope, believing in a loving, friendly universe, even when evidence shows us otherwise. Strive for forgiveness when it seems impossible, and take every opportunity to be the most loving expression of God in the world.

Love is what you are, eternal, strong, and powerful.
Our true power always lies in our capacity to love one another.

Going Through the Motions

INTENTION SETTING

Back in the mid 2000's, Nintendo came out with a motion-controlled video gaming system called the Wii. My kids were young then, and it was our family's highly anticipated big Christmas present. The system had remote controls with wireless sensors that we held in our hands, and they connected with and controlled our character players on the screen. One program, Wii Fit, had games that encouraged physical activity. Specifically, I remember there was a running game we could play, and we were supposed to hold the controller in our hands while jogging in place in our living room. Our character on the screen would run a marathon race through all these different scenes, while burning calories, earning points, and beating opponents.

One day I walked into my living room to discover my youngest daughter lying on the floor, flat on her back with the Wii remote in her hand. She was playing the Wii Fit running game, shaking the remote in her hand back and forth aggressively, while watching her character run on the screen. She was cheating! She wasn't running at all. (I'll admit that part of me was secretly impressed that my 6-year-old had figured out how to outsmart the game all on her own.

Something about that "Gen Z" attitude of "work smarter, not harder," does seem innate!) Another part of me was so disappointed. She was just going through the motions to play the game! Was she getting points and winning? Technically, yes, but she was getting virtually no exercise at all. Why was that even fun for her?

It felt like a great analogy for our spiritual life. Often, we get on the spiritual bandwagon. We take classes, attend services, volunteer, read books, dive into our spiritual practice daily, and so on. We are actively engaged, feeling the presence of God, and growing in consciousness. Other times, (and we have all been there) we are just going through the motions. We might still be doing those things — showing up for church, doing our spiritual practice, but something is different. We aren't as engaged. We're "shaking the remote" while lazily resting on our spiritual backs. The difference is subtle, but the meaning is clear. Going through the motions may get results, but what kind of results?

When she was lying down on the floor, my daughter's game character was traveling a great distance, earning points to win, but those results were kind of empty, not as meaningful, and certainly less impactful than if she had been playing the game the way it was intended. If she had been actively engaged, running in place the entire time, she would have felt very different end results in her body and in her being. The same is true for our spiritual life. When we fully commit with the intention of connecting to Source, engaging, listening, receiving etc., we feel the results in our being. We think creatively and recognize our good is already at hand. We see demonstrations in our life experiences. Again, the difference is subtle.

I offer this without judgement or criticism. It is meant as an opportunity for observation. Sometimes, we need spiritual tune-ups — a moment to step back and observe our relationship with God. So, check in with yourself...

Are you just going through the motions in your spiritual life?

Water You Saying?

SPEAKING OUR WORD

"Sticks and stones may break my bones,
but words can never hurt me!"

That is a LIE! Sticks and stones can break your bones, but I think we all know that words can also cause all kinds of damage. They are powerful. Words are the first step in creation. "In the beginning was the WORD" (John 1:1). Remember? All of creation was spoken into being. Knowing that we are made in the image and likeness of God, we — as individuals — reproduce this creative power. We create through our language. God's creative power... is also our power. We can potentially cause great harm with our words. That is the other side of this — we are creating either way, positively or negatively, whether we are aware of this spiritual law or not.

Unfortunately, many people misuse their word, particularly when it comes to children. Mothers, fathers, teachers, ministers, people in positions of authority can influence children's beliefs with their words. Children believe everything adults say. That is beautiful and scary at the same time. For instance, if we are told repeatedly that we are stupid as a child, we grow up believing that about ourselves. The flip side of this is that if we are told as a child that we are brilliant, smart, and can do anything, we grow up believing that. Our words to others are powerful because they create beliefs in them. Our words to ourselves are powerful because they create a belief in us. We know it is done unto us as we believe, so this is worth paying attention to from a spiritual perspective.

My favorite illustration of this spiritual principle — that our words have power — is the work of Masaru Emoto. He was the Japanese scientist who studied water molecules and became famous for photographing the crystals that formed in water. He published the photos in several books. You probably already know that the human body is about 70 percent water, but did you know a human fetus early on in its development is as much as 99% water? Life began for all of us as little watery gooballs. Talk about being the essence of life!

Emoto knew that water expresses itself. He wanted to find a way to see this and document it, so that's why he began freezing the water and photographing the crystals that formed. The first thing he discovered was that the water responded to the vibrations of different kinds of music. Water that was exposed to classical music formed beautiful, elegant crystals. The water that was exposed to violent heavy metal music with negative lyrics formed fragmented and deformed crystals — or no crystals at all. The negative song lyrics got him thinking about the vibration of words and the message they convey. So, he wrote words and phrases on paper and wrapped the paper around bottles of water. Sounds crazy, right? Water can't read. His approach was very much: "let's just see what happens."

What he found was that water exposed to words like "Love" and "Gratitude" created attractive, well-formed crystals. Water exposed to negative expressions like "I can't do it!" Or name calling like "You fool!" either barely formed crystals or they were fragmented and broken. His point was this: "the vibration of good words has a positive effect on our world, whereas the vibration from negative words has the power to destroy."[1] I wonder if he realized he was demonstrating spiritual law?

Emoto worked with the water in petri dishes or bottles inside a laboratory. I wonder about the water in plants, trees, animals, lakes, rivers, the oceans, the ground, and our human bodies. All of it is an endless opportunity for vibrational effect. It's like that meme that circles around various social media platforms that says: If speaking kindly to plants helps them grow, imagine what speaking kindly to humans can do?

Emoto's research showed us that water is always listening and creating. Whatever word we use for the Power behind everything... God, Spirit, Universe, Source, Life... it is always listening. In The Science of Mind® Ernest Holmes says, "It is as though there were a Universal Ear, listening to and hearing everything that we say, feel, or think, and reacting to it."[2] With our speech, we have the power to create beauty and harmony for ourselves and the world or... we can create chaos and destruction. Which one we create depends on how mindful we want to be with our speech.

There seems to be a gap between the point when we intellectually understand the power of our words... and the point when we are so mindful of it that we implement it and apply it effectively. Most people are probably somewhere in that gap. I am very aware of this principle, and I fail at applying it pretty much every day. But that doesn't mean I stop trying. We always have the free will and choice to think new thoughts and speak new words. We can choose to speak of our joys, our gratitude, and our love. We can claim our highest good, even before we see it. That is the best time to do it. <u>The more we believe our words are powerful, the more powerful our words become</u>. I underlined that line because it is important. That is what faith is.

We can never underestimate our ability to be transformed by the renewing of our minds in each new day, really in each moment. So just in case you find yourself accidentally complaining, speaking negatively to yourself or others, try not to give in to the natural inclination to judge yourself as a failure, but instead... gently, lovingly, make the decision and the choice right then in that moment to speak differently. Spirit within you is always listening, and that is exciting. It is a great responsibility, yes, but even more so, it is a tremendous opportunity!

How would you speak if you knew that Life within you
was always listening, always creating?
What would you declare about your life?
What would you affirm about yourself and others?

A Guided Communion Meditation

COMMUNION/COMMUNING WITH GOD

A couple years ago, I attended a lengthy, all-day church visioning workshop. The topic was vague and a little boring, and ideas were either from left-field or non-existent. Enthusiasm was waning, and by the end of the first hour, I started questioning the spiritual productivity of our gathering. Looking around as the day went on, I could tell a lot of other people felt the same way. Then, our leader did something strange.

In the middle of this meeting, he decided to hold the Eucharist. That's right. He decided we all needed to have Holy Communion. I looked at my empty plate and everyone else's. We'd already eaten our catered lunch of deli sandwiches and chips. Most of us had already eaten some of the homemade dessert a volunteer brought. The plate of those leftover brownies was still on the food table. He grabbed it and said, "This will work. We're sharing a meal together. A brownie can be a meal. Everybody take a piece of brownie. Use whatever drink you have."

This was without a doubt the most loosey-goosey approach to the elements I had ever experienced. I personally thought he had lost his mind. But then he started talking and reminded us about the

Lord's supper, the words Jesus spoke, the concept of breaking bread — oops, "breaking brownie" — together as a group of like-minded believers. By the time we got to "... this we do in remembrance of Him," it actually seemed okay. Don't get me wrong, it was weird, but the Spirit was there. The essence, meaning, and power behind the ritual was there. Holy Communion is ritual commemoration. It somehow worked.

The whole scene made me think about eating in general, regarding our "communion with the Divine." Could we use our regular daily food as our own private communion-style ritual? Could eating a meal while thinking about our connection to God become a spiritual practice, a method, a way to "commune" with God, Spirit, the Universe, Source? Was it really that much different than saying grace, blessing our meal, or giving thanks for our food?

So, I gave it a try, and guess what? It was strange, but it worked. So, if you have an open mind, I created this Personal Guided Communion Meditation. You can certainly try this when you are eating alone, but there is also something to be said for families and friends gathered around a table, experiencing this together.

Please note: this unique, progressive, spiritual practice exercise is in no way meant to belittle, change, or disrespect the Eucharist, Holy Communion, or the Lord's Supper. I appreciate a reader's willingness to explore new ways to practice faith.

Step 1: Breathe

When your meal is prepared and ready before you, take a moment to get comfortable in your seat. Close your eyes. Pay attention to your breathing for a few seconds. Just notice it. Take a nice deep breath. Maybe hold it for a few seconds, then exhale and release it. For right now, make your breath just a little bit deeper than normal. Do that a few times and then let your breathing return to normal. Relax. Enjoy a moment of gratitude for your lungs doing the job they do, breathing for you.

. . .

Step 2: Your Health

Put your hand on your heart. Have gratitude for your heart beating without you having to think about it. Imagine it glowing and spreading good energy through your body with perfect health, moving positive healing energy to all your body systems, all your organs, to every cell in your body. Consider all the healthy decisions you make for your body. Think of the healthy choices you make with the food and drink that you put in your body for nourishment. Rest in that for a moment, the amazing way your body works — the way you are able to take in food and drink for nourishment of your perfect, functioning body.

Step 3 The Metaphor

Jesus used the concept of nourishment at the last supper. He used food and drink, the bread and the wine, as the metaphor for us to remember him, to remember not only his presence, but his teachings which were based on love and unity. We eat and drink to nourish our own physical bodies. With the same reverence, respect, and contemplation, you can take in the food and drink before you to also nourish your spirit, your true essence beyond your physical body... your soul.

Step 4: Receive.

Rest your hands in your lap a moment, with the palms facing up, in a position of acceptance, in a position of receiving. This is not church communion with the bread and the cup. This is your conscious communion with your Divine Source. Let that fill you. Let that nourish you. Let that radiate through your soul. Receive and accept this love, this connection with God, your Divine Source.

In the same way you imagined your body glowing with radiant

health, imagine your entire soul aglow with this nourishing gift. And when you do this, think of all the other souls who participate in the communion ritual, whether in a church, spiritual center, or at a table in their homes. Celebrate your unity and oneness with them.

And so it is. Amen.

Communion with the Divine, no matter how it is practiced, invites and reveals more good in our life experience.

The Cheerful Receiver

LAW OF CIRCULATION

The Law of Circulation is about giving and receiving, reaping what we sow, and living in the flow of abundance. The Bible reminds us in 2 Corinthians 9:6-7 that God loves a cheerful giver. I would venture to say that God also enjoys a cheerful receiver. Receiving is just as vital a part of the equation, yet some of us get weird about cheerfully accepting our good. What does that even mean? Think about what it means to be a receiver.

I'm probably the last person who should try to use a football analogy, but here goes. What does the person in the receiver position do? His job is to catch the ball without dropping it, falling, or getting knocked down. How does he do this? Receivers run so fast, and their eyes are always on the ball or on the quarterback throwing the ball. Where are their hands? Receivers almost always run with their arms stretched out in front of them and their hands wide open — ready to catch that ball. Ready to receive! That's what it means to be a receiver — being ready to receive.

Open hands are the key to the law of circulation,
in both directions.

We should always have hands that are ready to give and ready to receive. If we are clutching at things and holding on too tightly to what we have while we are trying to receive our good, it doesn't work. We are not in the flow. Sometimes that means we have to make room for our good, both mentally and physically. Nature abhors a vacuum. When we create a state of emptiness or lack, nature will immediately move to fill it. Getting ready to receive means creating a vacuum mentally, by being still, quieting our thoughts, meditating, praying, etc., and physically, by making space for our good that is coming our way. That means looking around our lives to see if we need to make some room.

Steve Harvey tells a wonderful story about when he was young and still living at home. He told his mom every day when he came home from work that he was going to save up and get a new car, but she kept reminding him that his old broken-down junk car was still in the yard, sitting there. He was getting discouraged. She finally told him he had no room for this great new car he was envisioning! He had to make room for it. The Universe had no place to put his new car until he cleared a space for it.

In Steve Harvey's case, he got rid of a car to make room for another car, but often the things we give are completely unrelated to the things we end up receiving. It's not about the things, it's about the cycle, the flow, and the movement. The moment you decide to create the space for your good is when you know it is on the way. Everything is connected in Spirit. Everything is connected, period. Everything has energy. Everything is part of the flow of the law of circulation.

I invite you to play with the concept. Ask yourself, what can you let go of, and what can you release? You could empty out a closet in your house, drop some stuff off at a thrift store, and end up with unexpected income the following week, or meet the person who offers you your dream job. We don't always know what good we will get when we are preparing to receive, but we know it is coming because that is the way the law works. It's not called the "possibility of circulation" or the "potentiality of circulation." It's called the LAW of circulation. The law does not expect you to give without receiving in return, somewhere, somehow. Be willing to play with this spiritual principle and have fun with your receiving!

Play with the law of circulation.
Cheerfully make room for your good!

In Sickness or Health

RECOGNIZING HEALTH AND WHOLENESS

Y ears ago, during my Foundations of Science of Mind class, Beth, one of my instructors, said something very peculiar that I've never forgotten. Beth is a licensed spiritual practitioner, and she told us a story about Jan, one of her coworkers from her day job. Jan was going to be traveling on an airplane for a vacation, and she had been complaining to Beth about the trip, saying things like: "Every time I fly on an airplane, I get sick. It never fails. Somebody around me is always sick, and I catch it! I always end up sick when I travel."

Beth told us she let Jan finish complaining, and then she quietly smiled at her and replied, "Oh, really? I don't believe in sickness." The coworker rolled her eyes and sighed. That was not what she wanted to hear.

At the time, I was new to New Thought philosophies and The Science of Mind®, and I was a little stunned at Beth's comment. Frankly, she sounded nuts! Her coworker probably thought she sounded nuts, too. Could you imagine actually saying to another person, "I don't believe in sickness?" We all know sickness is a real thing. We see it every day. People catch things. (Hello, Covid? The flu?) Viruses spread. People are diagnosed with diseases. Sickness is a condition of life we have all seen and experienced in varying degrees and on some level. It happens.

But does it have to?

What would happen if we opened ourselves to the idea that sickness is not a natural part of our human existence? What if "belief in sickness" is actually optional? What if choosing to think in this unique way is beneficial to our overall health and well-being? (Hint: It IS!)

I am not exactly a newbie to The Science of Mind® anymore, and I think I finally get what Beth was saying. By telling us the story of her coworker's comments, and her subsequent response, Beth was illustrating the concept of wholeness and the importance of vigilantly paying attention to our thoughts, beliefs, words, and expectations. The coworker was expecting sickness, talking about sickness, worried about fighting sickness. She was thinking about it, focused on it. It was on her mind. It was in her consciousness.

When we understand the spiritual truth of God's wholeness, of what is possible when we focus on the goodness of God, these kinds of thoughts about sickness simply do not belong in our consciousness. So what kind of thoughts do belong in our consciousness?

Remember the apostle Paul encouraged us to think a certain way: "Finally, brethren, whatever things are true, whatever things are noble, whatever things are right, whatever things are pure, whatever things are lovely, whatever things are of good report, if there is any virtue and if there is anything praiseworthy — meditate on these things" (Phil. 4:8).

He told us to meditate on these things. Think about these things. What kind of things? Things that are true, noble, right, pure, love, good report, virtuous, praiseworthy.

Where does sickness fit into all that? It doesn't. Sickness is not any of those things. We know we are to affirm good things for ourselves and for others. The coworker was affirming for herself the idea of getting sick — to the point she was expecting it! It doesn't matter if that's what happened in the past. (Even I once got a head cold after traveling on an airplane.)

Our past experiences cannot dictate our transformation through the renewing of our minds. Remember, Paul told us in Romans 12:2: "Do not conform to the pattern of this world, but be transformed by the renewing of your mind. Then you will be able to test and approve what God's will is — his good, pleasing and perfect will." It's not just about affirming good things. The next step is, we have to believe it. We must transform our minds to the point we believe.

I remember thinking a long time about Beth telling her coworker: "I don't believe in sickness," and thinking to myself — I could never say something that bold and unusual! What would people think? But deep down, I secretly wanted to be like my spiritual practitioner teacher. I wanted to not only speak my spiritual Truth confidently, but I wanted to live it! I wanted to be my authentic self and not worry what others might think of me. At this point in my spiritual journey, I see that when my inner consciousness believes something beyond a shadow of a doubt, the law responds. Period. That is what matters most — not how others might respond. Spiritual law is about me choosing to work on my own consciousness, every day, and the subsequent good that is revealed because of it. My thoughts and beliefs create my world. What I think about and focus on, I attract into my life. So, can you say it with me?

I don't believe in sickness. I believe in health.

The Ladder: A Guided Meditation

MEDITATION

In the interest of opening your mind to a moment of spiritual contemplation, what follows is a written guided meditation for your consideration. Reading a guided meditation may seem counter intuitive, but sometimes just relaxing, taking in the words, and visualizing them in your mind can produce a powerful meditative experience. Once you have read through it, you can return to this practice on your own simply by thinking about and imagining the experience again. For now, take a few minutes to sit or lie down somewhere that you won't be disturbed and consider this...

Imagine it is a beautiful sunny warm day. You are standing outside on the softest green grass. It is bug-free and lush. You take off your shoes and feel very grounded and one with the earth. You also feel a little heavy and very human, standing there — maybe even a little weighed down by life. Before you, seemingly out of nowhere, appears a ladder. This is not like any ordinary ladder. The legs of this ladder go straight into the earth, solidly. You look up, and the ladder is so tall, you cannot tell where it ends or even IF it ends. It goes clear up into the sky, past the puffy white clouds, on into the heavens forever.

Because you are inexplicably drawn to this ladder, you step up onto the first rung. It is sturdy and steady, and it's as if you are magnetically connected to it, like it is really an extension of yourself. Immediately, you sense that this ladder is magical, and climbing it feels like a very good idea. This is a refuge, a sanctuary. It feels like this ladder is a way to connect to your inner self.

Instinctively, you step up a couple more rungs — just a few feet off the ground. You feel that human heaviness weighing you down, though, and it doesn't jive with the magical charm of the ladder. So, you begin to metaphorically empty out your pockets. You release the things your ego thinks you should hold on to, you know — your worries, your struggles, your fears, your imagined problems, your knots. You simply drop them to the ground below you. Imagine each one dropping to the ground with a thud.

Empty yourself of it all, whether it is the job you don't like, the fight you had with your sister, the nagging cough you have had for a week, the unexpected bills that showed up in the mail, or the current news story that is breaking your heart. Your pockets are deep. Only you know what needs to be released in this moment. You suddenly realize you have been holding onto a lot, and you don't have to anymore! Whatever the worries are — choose to release them all right here, right now, and rise up this sturdy ladder. This is your focus... to rid yourself of what weighs you down so you can get on with the great idea of climbing this ladder.

With your pockets completely emptied, your mind clear, and your intention set, it is so much easier now to keep climbing. You are lighter, and you have absolutely no fear of falling at all because this ladder instills such a feeling of safety and security. You continue to rise at your own pace, and it is joyful and fun.

It isn't long before an intriguing feeling of peace fills you. You feel so light. You are up ridiculously high in the sky; there is still no fear associated with being this high. It is exhilarating! You feel expanded, like an open lens. It's the ladder... this magical ladder that is an extension of you. It dawns on you that this is where you really belong, up high on this ladder where the air is clean and clear. You love this feeling. You love thinking about this feeling. This, you realize, is what thinking "higher thoughts" means. This is where you are connected with the Divine, with your higher self, your truth. This is where you commune with, recognize, and sense the harmony and peace of the Source of all Life. Right here, there is love. Up here, you instinctively understand how loved and supported you are, and it feels amazing. You close your eyes, breathe in the moment, and smile.

Exhaling, you open your eyes. You can't believe you haven't noticed this until now, but all around you there are more ladders. Loved ones, acquaintances, strangers, are all standing on their own ladders! How did you not see them before? It occurs to you in a flash that of course everyone has their own ladder! Everyone has access to the Divine. Everyone is at a different place in their journey, at a different level of consciousness. Some people are far below you, still standing on the ground, refusing to take the first step onto the ladder. Some people are stuck on the first few rungs, unwilling or unable to divest themselves of that which weighs them down. Some are at the same level you are, and that makes you smile. Glancing upward, some people are quite far above you. They are illumined, experiencing an even higher level of understanding of their unity with the Divine. Everyone is at their own level, and that is okay. It's more than okay; it is perfect!

You feel so good that you want to take this feeling with you back into your life, back into your day. The best part of this experience is realizing that you can. This expansiveness, this love, this light fills your being. You slowly begin to climb back down, content in knowing the ladder is always here. It is an extension of your heart and therefore always accessible. Smile as you imagine your feet stepping back onto the soft green grass.

An imagined ladder can be your path, your practice,
and your channel to your truth — to your natural divinity.
Climb on up anytime you wish!

We, The Chosen

OBSERVING THOUGHTS AND BELIEFS

M any years ago, I read a poem by poet Gailmarie Pahmeier
called, "The Wife of Noah Comforts the Young Bride of
Their Son." On particularly difficult news days, I still think about it.
In the short poem, Noah's wife has a conversation with their son's
wife about the severity of their situation. The world is being
destroyed. The daughter-in-law is scared and sad, doubting her part
in it all. Rightly so!

Noah's wife is calm, firm in her purpose and faith, and speaks like
a loving, comforting mother-in-law. She tells her how important they
are — the women. The final line is forever etched in my memory:

*"We'll be the reason for everything
after the rain."* [1]

Noah's wife is referencing the fact that no matter how severe the
destruction, they are being saved for a reason, and it will quite
literally be their job, their duty, their great privilege to repopulate the
Earth. It will only happen through them, the women. But she is
saying something more. She is saying that they are important, that

they are chosen for this mission that will take place after the flood and subsequent destruction.

I think it is okay to admit that we are living in fairly destructive times. I am the last person to ever talk about doomsday, end times, evil, or devastation. I don't believe in any of that. I believe God is good and only good, period. There is no duality and no presence of evil (other than our unfortunate, misguided choice to believe in one.) The goodness of God is ever present always — and we are not only ONE with this goodness, but expressions of it.

But, come on, we can all see the destruction happening around us. We are scared and confused. We doubt our part in it all. Who is "we?" Those of us with even the slightest bit of spiritual awareness, from the ordained minister, to the seat-filler filled with doubt in the pew on Sunday morning, and maybe most especially, those of us who consider ourselves to be "spiritual, but not religious." The spectrum of awareness is wide, and wherever we fall on it — we are chosen.

Here are a few situations currently making me crazy; perhaps they are weighing heavily on you, too:

- The political landscape in the United States is rather destructive. The lies. The pain. The corruption. The mistrust. The foreign meddling. The divisiveness, anger, and hate. It seems endless. We don't know what to believe anymore.

Breathe, stay calm. We are chosen.

- The fires, rain, flooding, storms, and earthquakes — it is as if the earth does not want us here anymore. Our leaders and corporate CEOs behave as if the Source of all Life is somehow pleased with the size of their personal bank accounts. Our children are outraged and terrified.

Breathe, one with Nature... We are chosen.

- The deadly Covid-19 virus outbreak locked down cities and entire nations, creating rampant worldwide fear. The virus killed. Vaccines were created. The virus subsided. It mutated. It returned. Fear, mistrust, and more fear. The Infinite Intelligence of the Universe operates within our physical bodies.

Rest in what you know to be true. We are chosen.

We can't help feeling exhausted and a little weary. We look to our leaders, we look to our elders, and these days, we see greed, incompetence, and fear. To whom can we turn? We know the answer. We turn to God, the One Spirit, the Universe, our one true Source. We turn to Love, because Love is what is real, and we express it as best we can. Love yesterday, love today, love again tomorrow. An endless loop. Wake, pray, love, repeat.

Dear ones, dear conscious ones... we are the ones who understand the Unity of all Life. We are the ones who know and trust in the Divine, who know and trust in our own divinity, who see that divinity in others. We must not lose hope. We are chosen to hold space for the devastated, to be the presence of love and light in the world, to teach forgiveness, and to hold fast to our spiritual truths. There can be no good vs. evil when we only believe in the Good. Goodness prevails, for there is no other way. We know this. Our good is revealed when we faithfully believe in it. There can be no other way. This devastation will end, and when it does, my friends, remember:

"We'll be the reason for everything after the rain."

Ask for the Truth–Then Believe It

UNITY WITH ALL LIFE

"The Truth of our unity, our oneness,
and our harmony must come to pass
because we believe in it."

I spoke these words once in a sermon. Goodness, they are lofty, optimistic words! You are probably left wondering how we do that. I have always been a fan of tangible, practical instructions. Give me a spiritual practice, a method of prayer, or an exercise to do. What can I do to help me shift my consciousness into knowing and believing this Truth of unity, oneness, and harmony?

I have an embarrassing personal story to illustrate this. I live in a regular neighborhood with lots of beautiful houses. I don't know all my neighbors, but we have a Facebook group page for my neighborhood, so I have gotten to know some of them from that. There is a person in my neighborhood whom I don't know, who has posted some comments in the group that I don't necessarily agree with or like. I know which house is his from his posts, so I know exactly where he lives, which is not far from me. During the 2020 election, this man had signs in his yard supporting a particular candidate that I did not support. I'll just leave it at that and spare you the details.

I walk my dog every day, and every day I walk by this person's house. I noticed that every time I walked by his house, I felt anger, frustration, and resentment toward this person whom I didn't even know. (I told you it's an embarrassing story.) I am a spiritual person, and this was really bothering me. Why was I feeling these feelings about someone I did not really know? What was I supposed to be learning from the situation?

I discovered long ago that negative experiences are never about the other person; they are about me. Life is always a reflection of our inner consciousness. Our inner world creates our outer world. I had to ask myself what was going on in me that was being reflected here. So, I took this problem to my spiritual practice, into my meditation, prayer, and spiritual mind treatment. I was seeking to know the Truth of this person, the Truth of our oneness and unity. I asked for this Truth to be revealed to me, because I believed it had to be there. You will never guess what happened.

A few nights later, I was walking my dog again, and I saw the man out mowing his lawn on his riding mower. Then I watched him ride off his lawn, into the road, across the street, over a couple houses, where he proceeded to mow the empty lot in the neighborhood. It may sound silly, but I swear, I almost cried. Spirit was showing me exactly what I needed to see. He was a good person! (You are probably thinking, of course he's a good person!) I am a good person. You are a good person; we are all good because the goodness of God is in all of us. It turns out I just needed to have that moment of recognition of that Truth. I needed to see his goodness right in front of me, and Spirit delivered. Real or imagined, I was in conflict with this person. Yet, there he was, just straight up doing a good deed, caring about the neighborhood looking nice, sharing his time, his talents, and his resources — giving them FREELY! He was doing a kind thing for others, and that is something I like to do! It is something on which we agree and something we have in common. Imagine that!

The moment got practically comical. While he was mowing, I walked past him with my dog, and he had this great big joyful smile on his face and waved at me, and I waved back, also smiling. There we were, smiling and waving like friendly neighborhood dorks. I was instantly freed of the bondage of anger, resentment, and discord. In that moment, I knew the Truth of who we both were.

It is a very "high consciousness" thought to believe in the truth of our oneness. It is a very "low consciousness" thought to separate ourselves into groups of Us and Them, as I had been doing. There are endless opportunities for us to live from our highest spiritual truth. We humans today are bombarded with messages of what is "real." There is an incessant push to make us believe that what we see and what we hear around us is the "truth" of life, that all these human reactions — fear, anger, resentment, and powerlessness — are the truth. They are not. We are one. Even though we may see all sorts of evidence to the contrary, we can still believe in and know the truth. Ultimately, we can be freed by it.

The truth is, we are all divine spiritual beings
having a human experience.
We are united in the Oneness of Spirit.

The Return to Normal

UNITY WITH ALL LIFE

When mandatory quarantines began to slowly lift during the global Covid-19 pandemic, there was a lot of talk about life "returning to normal" and what that might look like. With lockdowns, curfews, and self-imposed isolations, many people were justifiably going stir crazy, yet I kept wondering, to what, exactly, we were returning? What was "normal" anyway? One of my favorite sayings is:

"Normal is just a setting on a washing machine."

I love the analogy. Normal is just the way most of us were used to doing things — the way we lived life pre-pandemic. Was it a great way of doing things? Maybe for some. Maybe not for all. Okay, maybe not for most. Choice is the key, though — "normal" was our choice. If there is one thing the pandemic taught us, it's that there were other ways of doing things. Who would've thunk?

Maybe normal was just what we all tolerated without realizing we were merely tolerating it. Thanks to Covid-19 and the subsequent time of quarantined isolation, we were faced with new choices. New beginnings. Opportunities to start fresh and change our setting — to change the way we did things. That's right, the dreaded C-word everybody loves to hate: CHANGE.

Have you ever looked at the settings on your washing machine? Mine has four. Normal, (which I decided I'm done with) Heavy, Casual, and Delicate. I became intrigued by these other options and how they might relate to post-pandemic life. Stick with me, here...

We'll start with Heavy. On second thought, do we really want to go there? I was quarantined with my husband and seventeen-year-old daughter, a budding young baker who was well stocked with Costco-sized bags of flour and sugar. We had chocolate chip cookies, coconut cream pie, chocolate eclairs, brownies, white chocolate cranberry cookies, lemon merengue pie, cannoli, and on and on. She never stopped baking. Yes, my post-pandemic life has been heavy all right, but that's not the illustration I wish to discuss.

Looking back at what I refer to as "the lost Covid years," wasn't it a dark, depressing, and weighty time? The pandemic was a heavy burden for us all to bear, heavy with fear, illness, loss, grief, frustration, leading eventually to the polarization of masks, vaccines, and a virus. Why would we choose to carry the weight of all that disharmony into our future?

Moving on...

Let's look at Casual. I don't mean working from the couch in yoga pants and forgetting to put on a bra most days. (Wasn't that an interesting time for us all?) No, living a casual life means being more relaxed, calm, and serene in my mind. I don't know about you, but I could use more of that. My mind is where everything happens — my perceptions, my attitude, my outlook. I like the idea of not taking things so seriously, being more easy going. When we trust that life is good and that we are one with the Power and Presence of God, we are naturally going to be calmer and more peaceful. There is no need to return to the rushing, and the "busy"-ness. Choosing a casual life means being carefree, not in the sense of not caring, but carefree in the sense of being free from worry, free from fear. Wrinkle-free, if you will. Or, for the purpose of this book, knot-free! Casual life sounds perfectly delightful.

Then there is the rarely selected Delicate setting. When you wash your delicates, the washing machine is careful and gentle with your clothes. Being careful and gentle with our future sounds like an intelligent decision to me. It is a choice to make, not from a place of fear, but from a place of positive proactivity. The pandemic taught us to be conscientious and careful about our health with things like hand washing, hygiene, and the responsible care and protection of the elderly and immunocompromised. Those are habits that can easily become part of post-pandemic life. They do not have to be viewed as restricting, limiting, and burdensome.

I like the idea of being delicate with ourselves and others. Life after lockdown requires that we all have some patience. We learned to be cautious with our thoughts and beliefs, reluctant to give in to fear mongering and hype. We learned to be sensitive to the needs of others, while remembering to be gentle with ourselves. The delicate setting is a nice place to realize our Oneness. And speaking of Oneness, we saw how the earth thrives when humans shelter in place. It's my hope that we can all continue to be gentle with Mother Earth. It deserves some delicate treatment. Delicate life sounds amazing. We have options! We have settings other than "Normal."

Did you notice how creative people got during the pandemic — all of us working from home, sheltering in place, solving our problems in new ways? I mean, for heaven's sake, Saturday Night Live figured out how to present entire episodes with cast, crew, and musicians all quarantined in their respective homes. All kinds of problems got solved! Don't you wonder how outside-the-box life solutions can potentially be, living on whatever new setting we choose?

I find myself asking all kinds of questions about the post-pandemic future, as Covid-19 becomes a distant memory. Things like: What would happen if people continued working from home? Why can't we always limit our shopping trips to only when necessary? What if our educational system continued to be flexible and effective with online distance learning? Can we appropriately compensate our most important supply chain workers? Can we actually make decisions that are in the best interest of humanity, of All-Life? Is withdrawing from the world now and then beneficial to everyone's health and well-being, including planet Earth? What did we all really learn from this experience? There is certainly a lot to consider, moving forward. In the meantime, go check out your washing machine for inspiration.

How was your post-pandemic "return to normal?"
Is it time to consider a different setting for your life,
one that is more aligned with your good?

Freedom: Who Do We Think We Are?

UNITY WITH ALL LIFE

In her famous sonnet, "The New Colossus," Emma Lazarus personifies the Statue of Liberty as a welcoming figure, comforting and mother-like, emanating a worldwide greeting. Lady Liberty lifts her light beside the golden door, letting in "your tired, your poor, your huddled masses" who are yearning to be free. How majestic for those who arrived on ships through Ellis Island, to look up and see the massive, welcoming lady in the harbor! It is a poetic sentiment, one full of hope, opportunity, and compassion. It's the kind of thing we read about in a high school government class and for a hot minute we think about majoring in political science in college and running for public office because surely that's the right thing to do for this great nation!

Then again, maybe the language of the poem is a little idealistic and naive. After all, times have changed, haven't they? The poem was written over 130 years ago. Now we see scenes of desperate migrants and refugees deemed "illegal people," crossing rivers, risking death, incarceration, and the possibility of losing their children, all for a chance at freedom. The "tired... poor... huddled masses" still rings true for the images we see in the 2020s.

Immigration is an American value and part of our history. We are a nation of immigrants. As Marianne Williamson pointed out once, "If you're not descended from slaves who came from Africa or descended from Native Americans who were here for at least centuries before the white European settler came, who do you think you are?" It does make me wonder:

Who do we think we are?

I tend to see life's happenings through the lens of faith, not through the lens of political policy. I make no apologies for that. God teaches us to be compassionate, to be giving, and most importantly, to love. Full stop. But wait — there is more. Jesus taught, "Do unto others as you would have them do unto you" (Matt. 7:12). "Thou shalt love your neighbor as thyself" (Mark 12:31). "In as much as ye have done it unto one of the least of my brethren, ye have done it unto me" (Matt. 25:40).

So where does all this faith and scripture stuff fit into the broader context of God's people living harmoniously among the earth? Where does it leave us in the "border crisis?" And while we are on that subject, does God even recognize borders? The reality is that borders in general are a human-made concept. At some point we arbitrarily drew lines in the sand and said things like, "This is my continent, country, state, county, etc., and that is yours. Stay over there." When white European settlers arrived in what we now call America and began treating the land like a commodity to be owned, Native Americans were puzzled. They viewed the land as something to connect and live with, necessary for the survival and well-being of all, not something that could ever be claimed, owned, or divided. I get it — a country is a country, and an open border is not a border at all. It is an oxymoron. It's unrealistic to believe we can just let everyone in and collectively groove on down to the hippie compound celebrating our love, unity, and oneness.

Or is it?

That other pesky scripture keeps rolling around in my head: "With God, all things are possible" (Matt. 19:26). The sheer volume of people migrating to America through legal and non-legal channels is considered a problem for a lot of people. While I understand how it can cause difficult situations, I also know Spirit does not see problems, only solutions. God is bigger than any problem, and the more we focus on the human "problem," the worse it will get. We have seen that happen already. I am certainly not suggesting we ignore it, either! Perhaps we can shift our focus and start believing in a solution that includes and incorporates us loving our neighbor and doing unto others as we would have them do unto us. Let us start with just the belief in that possibility. Maybe both sides of the political public policy aisle can start there, with a belief in the possibility.

The 4th of July is the day we commemorate our nation's birth and celebrate our personal freedom. Freedom is a quality of the divine and therefore a birthright of all children of God, regardless of citizenship. We can choose to see the immigrant and undocumented not as threats, but as brothers and sisters whose dignity is tied to our own dignity, whose lack of freedom calls into question our own freedom. Just how free are we? If today we are caging the migrant child, who will we imprison tomorrow?

Ernest Holmes reminds us in The Science of Mind® that "True liberty comes only through true harmony; true harmony only through true unity; and true unity can come only through the conscious realization that we are one with God or Good."[1]

Paraphrased, it could read like this: We can get along with everyone, including the immigrant. We are one with the immigrant, so we must treat them well. Also, you, the immigrant, and I are all one with God — who can only be Goodness.

In the meantime, a prayer:

Knowing and trusting that there is only One Great Spirit of God, we declare our individual oneness and unity with It. Let our eyes be opened to the possibility of the grace within us dissolving our human, ego-based, manufactured problems. May we be reminded that every soul is born of God's goodness. What we want for ourselves, let us want and declare as true for everyone. We ask for help seeking the good of all and fully expect to experience its unfoldment. Let us see the Divine in every soul and consciously operate from a place of love. Solutions, abundance, and intelligence are present in this moment. We give great thanks for the continuous opportunity to show up as God's unconditional love in this world. And So It Is. Amen.

Who do we think we are?
One with God, one with our Good.
Each individually, all collectively.

It's Fine

SEEKING PEACE

My three daughters are similar in many ways, but each has her own unique personality, traits, and skills. The youngest one has always behaved very differently than her older sisters. I have found spiritual inspiration in her unique approach to life. When the older girls were little, they worried about being dressed just right and paid a lot of attention to their hair. They worked hard in school to get good grades, almost to the point of perfectionism. If anyone pointed out that they had done something wrong or criticized them, they got upset.

The youngest one — didn't. She never worried or got upset about anything. From the time she was very little, this trait was quite dominant in her little personality. As soon as she learned to talk, conversations went like this:

MOM: "Honey, your shoes are on the wrong feet."
YOUNGEST: "It's fine."

MOM: "Your shirt is on backwards."
YOUNGEST: "It's fine."

MOM: "Your teacher says your handwriting is a little messy. Maybe you can try harder to be neat?"
YOUNGEST: "It's fine."

You get the idea, on and on. Everything was fine in this child's world, even when by my standards or someone else's, it wasn't. I had never noticed what a huge part of her life this sentiment was. Then she became a teenager, and she was saying it even more...

MOM: "Honey, your room is a mess. Why don't you pick it up?"
YOUNGEST: "It's fine."

MOM: "Where are your glasses?"
YOUNGEST: "They're probably at school somewhere — It's fine."

MOM: "Did you study for your history test?"
YOUNGEST: "Nah — but it's fine."

I would try to push her to care more about her grades, how she presented herself, keeping up with her belongings, etc., and I was always met with (you guessed it) "It's fine." We would go a few rounds when I wanted the dishes done at a certain time, demanded something be picked up immediately, or expected her to generally do what she was told!

Secretly, I used to worry this was the laziest kid on earth who didn't care about anything. But then I started to notice something interesting. This kid had a sense of peace and serenity within her that I never saw in her sisters, and frankly, I don't see in many adults. It is beautiful, and I am a little jealous of it.

This kid does not let things get to her or bother her. She is perfect just the way she is, and she knows it. The way she does things is perfect, too, and she knows it. It is as if she has instinctively always known what is important and what really matters. As spiritual seeking adults, can we say the same? I think for this kid, "It's fine" is the secular equivalent to "Trust in the Lord with all your heart" (Prov. 3:5). "It's fine" is her version of "It is well with my soul." "It's fine" is her mantra for "Why should my heart be troubled?"

She trusts life. She is affirming good things for herself. She is declaring her intention that all is well for her. She believes "It's fine," all the time. As much as I want to instill responsibility, awareness, and effort as a parent, I am also starting to see the value in cultivating a peaceful sense of knowing that "It's fine." In a way, she is teaching me to consider what worries I can release. I can do things differently than the people around me. It is refreshing. As her mom, I have always joked that this girl effortlessly "Forrest Gumps" her way into blessings, opportunities, and abundance. It is clear to me that her peaceful, easygoing nature plays an important role in the revelation of her good. Perhaps we should all be so genuinely carefree in our faith and belief. It might just do wonders for our life experience.

Where in your life can you step back
and even just for moment,
stop and say: "It's fine...?"
(Because maybe it is!)

Miracle Living

GRATITUDE

I am a little embarrassed to admit this, but... I don't know how to grow things. I have never had a garden. My family says I'm not allowed to have house plants anymore because the few times I have tried, it ended badly for the plants. So, this is just something I have accepted about myself. I am an adult. I am not a planter-gardener type person. I'm okay with it.

When the Covid-19 pandemic began and we were all on lockdown quarantine, I started noticing that sometimes I was unable to get everything I wanted from the grocery store. Like many people, I started thinking about the supply chain and specifically, how I get my food. I realized that I am pretty dependent on the grocery store! (As I said, a farmer I am not.) I wasn't panicked or scared; I have complete faith in our food supply chain. My inconvenience was minimal. I just started thinking about whether I could grow something I could actually eat. How would one even learn to do such a thing?

During World War I and World War II, when some foods were rationed and it was harder to get fruits and vegetables, people began planting "Victory Gardens." At its peak in 1943, there were 18 million victory gardens in the United States! Surely some of those people had never grown their own plants before. The most intriguing part, to me, was that these gardens were considered a "morale booster" in that people could feel empowered and rewarded for their efforts. That made me want to try it even more. I was all for a "morale boost" during the pandemic.

Having literally no experience gardening, I ordered some seeds, potting soil, and starter pots from a home improvement store's website. Let me be clear about my intention: I was not attempting to plant a garden to feed myself and my family. My approach was more childlike intrigue, as in: "Can I actually do this? Let's have fun and see what happens!" I viewed the whole thing as an experiment in positivity, a way to challenge myself, and a life-affirming spiritual exercise during my first ever global pandemic.

You will never guess what happened! (Or maybe you can — you probably learned how to grow plants in the 4th grade like a normal person.) My seeds sprouted! Every single one of them! Within just a few days, there were tiny little green seedlings popping up from the soil. I had tears in my eyes the first time I saw them. My own little plant babies! What a miracle! Which leads me to my point...

I really did see it as a miracle! Life is full of very good things that we can at any point refer to as miracles. A quote often attributed to Albert Einstein says, "There are only two ways to live your life: One is as though nothing is a miracle. The other is as though everything is a miracle." There are so many miracles all around us, every day. There is so much good to notice, recognize, and acknowledge. My gardening experiment was a terrific reminder of this.

- I put a seed in some dirt and give it some water, and it sprouts and grows into a plant that will eventually produce food. That's a miracle!
- Two random people meet, fall in love and have a baby. Textbook creation at its finest. That is a miracle!

- Every one of us is a walking miracle. Our hearts beat 100,000 times a day without us doing a thing to help it, sending blood to all our body systems and organs, which all function perfectly for optimal, balanced health. Talk about a walking miracle!
- I open an app on my cell phone, click a button, and suddenly I am video chatting with Grandma, sitting in her room, across the country. The internet, cell phones, apps... those are modern day miracles!
- Outside temperatures soar to a miserable 100 degrees, but inside, it is cool and comfortable. Air conditioning (and don't forget heat during the winter) is an absolute miracle.
- A deadly virus spreads around the world, but teams of scientists, researchers, and medical doctors develop a vaccine that helps lessen the severity and magnitude of the illness. What a miracle!

Our challenge is to live our lives as if we are surrounded by our good and everything is a miracle. We may start to look and sound crazy, but we also might feel better about the world and our place in it by viewing things this way. Believing that our experiences are miraculous, no matter how mundane, helps us naturally lean toward gratitude, and gratitude increases happiness!

Look for the miracles all around you. Acknowledge your good.
Give thanks and celebrate!

Formless Form: A Guided Meditation

MEDITATION

Sometimes all it takes to experience a deeply moving meditation session is the power of your imagination. Sit or lie down and take a few deep, relaxing breaths. Imagine you are comfortably lying on your bed with your eyes closed, drowsy, and ready for rest. Your breath is slow and even, lulling you into a deep and pleasant slumber. Picture this scene. As if you are having some sort of out-of-body, dreamlike experience, imagine that your inner sense of life, your being, starts to rise up — not as if you are dying or separating from your body, but as if you are existing in both places simultaneously. Your inner being rises all the way up to the ceiling, just floating. You look down and see yourself sleeping peacefully on the bed.

You no longer feel the restrictions of your physical body, and that excites you. You are simply being in a different form, existing and taking up space without any physical limits. You realize that because of your new formless form, you can continue to rise and make your way through the ceiling of your bedroom, through the top of your home. You look down at the roof. You continue to gently float higher. There is no sense of fear because there is no body that can fall. You are simply a being of peace and light, wholeness, floating with a feeling of total safety. You continue to rise over your neighborhood, and now you can see the entire city in which you live.

You see treetops, streets, homes, and businesses. Going higher still, you see other nearby cities and communities. Now, notice that you are looking at the state you live in, and eventually, observe that your view has widened to include the entire country and continent. The landmass is enormous! Rise so high into the clouds and stars that you can see the whole planet — oceans, islands, continents, and even the moon. You are so high, but there is no fear from this place where you are. There is only a sense of love and wholeness — a secure sense of *being-ness*, as you rise even higher. You can see other planets and the sun. You realize that you are now in the ethers, among the stars in the universe. You rise higher still and realize there is no longer any reason to seek out that tiny earth planet where your physical body is. It is inconsequential and frankly, not of any interest. This is of interest — being this formless form, because you are an expansive presence in the universe, of the universe, in God, of God.

This sense of loving wholeness, this *being-ness* that is within you, operating as you, is vibrating light. You realize in an instant that you are a pulsing point of light in the giant web and network that is "capital L" Life. You always were this point of light. You always are. It all begins to make sense. You are an expression of God's light in this infinite web. You realize that this is your true self. You feel a wave of comforting warmth wash through you and over you because this is the truth of your being, and it is so powerful! It is such a relief to feel this sense of expansion. Higher and higher, wider and wider. Nothing can restrict you, contain you, or limit you. Your true self is complete, unlimited wholeness. You are not just a being. You *are Being*. You are light. Breathe into and accept this knowing, this truth of who and what you are. This is the true nature of your very soul, your God-presence. Life-and-Light-in-action. Always. It cannot end. It cannot die. It simply IS.

Take as long as you like, enjoying this moment, before mentally traveling back through the universe, to our solar system, the sun and the stars and the clouds, back into earth's atmosphere. Imagine you float all the way back, and see your country, your state and community, your city, your neighborhood, and home, all the way back through your ceiling, into your bedroom, back into your body with a gentle, soft blending. You are still sleeping soundly. You notice the peaceful rhythm of your heartbeat — that pulsing, beating, electrical vibration. Reassurance comes over you because it is the same pulsing vibration you felt all the way out into the universe. It is a gentle reminder of the truth of your being.

The power of Life force energy is within you,
ever expanding, ever existing, in you, through you, as you.
It is good to meditate on this.

Summer Peach of Prosperity

PROSPERITY/ABUNDANCE AS SPIRITUAL PRINCIPLE

Have you ever tasted a deliciously elusive, perfect, summer peach? Do you know the kind I am talking about? Not too hard, not too soft. Sweet and juicy. The kind of peach that when you get one, you immediately want to go back to the store and buy ten more because it's THAT good. I enjoyed one recently. Not only was this peach delicious, but it was a perfect illustration of prosperity in action! After completing a 12-week class about prosperity consciousness and deepening spiritual awareness, I started seeing illustrations of prosperity everywhere!

When you hear prosperity, do you immediately think: Money? Cash? Your bank account? Material possessions? Income? Greed? I used to think of those things. Then I came to understand prosperity as a divine principle, spiritual law, and a naturally occurring process. Prosperity is a demonstration of Life (a.k.a. GOD in action!)

Join me on a grateful journey of prosperity mindfulness... After wiping the peach juice from my mouth and washing my hands, I couldn't help but wonder... where did this delicious peach come from? Why was it so delicious? How did I end up with it? The answer I kept hearing was: It's all God. And it's all Prosperity.

If you will forgive my oversimplification... Peaches grow on trees. Peach trees are planted from a seed. The peach I ate was born of a tree that was ultimately born from a single seed — (probably planted a long time ago.) You already know I am not much of a farmer, but from my rudimentary understanding, the process goes something like this: Seed, ground, water, sunshine, seedling, growth, plant, tree, fruit, harvest. THAT is the prosperity, abundance, and wisdom of nature. It is God-in-action. It is intelligent, and it is perfect.

But this miracle didn't happen without human help. After all, a farmer had to plant the seed. The farmer is Life, God-in-action. Farms have employees and workers — more Life, more God-in-action. These humans tend to the plants, nurture the trees, and grow the fruits of their labor. It is Life. It is Prosperity. They are paid for their work, so some good old fashioned "money" prosperity is also part of the process.

Eventually, the peaches are picked by workers. They are collected and packaged and transported. Someone loads them into a flat, onto a pallet, and into a truck. They are transported to fruit stands, farmers markets, grocery stores, moved across state lines, put on airplanes, and maybe even shipped to other countries.

The peaches are received at their destination. They are displayed and sold in stores, by more workers, also being paid for their work. More Life is involved; more participants take part in this divine practice of prosperity. Hours worked. Wages earned. Product produced. Produce sold.

I have always loved the way language works. PRODUCE. It is a noun: produce — as in, a peach is produce. Produce is a section of a grocery store. It is also a verb: as in, if nature does its work; if humans work and tend to these plants and trees, they produce. Can it be any clearer? It is growth, expansion, and creation. Prosperity. It is the natural way life works.

The peaches are ultimately purchased. I am blessed to write in an air-conditioned office, not work on a farm, outdoors, with hot summer temperatures. I am blessed to earn money for my work. I am prosperous. I spend some of my money on delicious peaches. I receive money; I give money. I give. I receive. As more juice drips down my chin (because of course I went to the store for more peaches) I recognize it as the joyful juice of a prosperous life. I am grateful, and life is good.

How do you take part in the divine prosperity process?

Dorothy's Shoes

UNITY WITH THE DIVINE

C onfession time. When I was a kid, I hated the movie *The Wizard of Oz*. I mean, I HATED it. As a highly sensitive empath long before I ever understood what that even meant, that wicked witch and those alien flying monkeys were terrifying — the stuff of nightmares! I have since gotten past my childhood fears and now fully appreciate the movie and the story. As an adult, I have discovered some deep spiritual wisdom in the film. For me, it boils down to just one meaningful symbol: It's about the SHOES.

Oh, those ruby red slippers. Fast forward to the end of the film — I am sure you remember. Yes, Dorothy had the power all the time! It has taken me years of metaphysical and spiritual training to begin to grasp this truth for my life. The shoes were always with her; she had them all along. The power of God, Spirit, Universe, Source is always within us!

Do you feel a "but..." coming? Yes, the power is always within us, but... we must DO something with this power. Quite a few things, actually...

The first thing we must do is recognize it. It took Dorothy the whole movie to realize she had the power within her to get what she wanted. That long, drawn-out journey with such a wonderful cast of characters led her to understanding and recognizing her own power. It doesn't matter that it is Good ol' Glinda who points it out to her at the end of the movie. ("You've always had the power, my dear...") Dorothy still had to recognize it for herself.

Have you recognized the power within you? This doesn't have to be a profoundly big religious thing. I personally like recognizing the power as simply the One Mind, One Energy, or One Life-Force back of all things. I call it God, and I know it to be good, period. Whatever you call it — the point is, this power just IS. Period. I try to recognize that in my life every day.

The next thing we have to do is really connect with this power — in fact, I would say, unify with it. We have to understand that the shoes are never coming off. We are a part of them, and they are a part of us. No wicked witch is coming to take them from us, and the flying monkeys sent to terrorize us aren't real. (I personally think we send our own monkeys, but that is a story for another day.) There is nothing we can do to separate ourselves from the love and power of God. We cannot be separated from our Good unless we do it ourselves through false beliefs and fears.

The third thing we have to do is believe. We must have faith in this power and believe in it enough to spur us into action. If we truly believe that the power of God is fully supporting us in every way, what might we do differently in our lives? If we really believe God is real, what risks might we take? This power present within us is both our constant companion and our natural ability to manifest our desires — all rolled into one. As I write in my journal repeatedly: "I am never alone. I always have God, and God always has me. God expresses through and as me."

The last thing we are meant to do with Dorothy's shoes is to click our little heels! Clicking your heels is the equivalent to stepping out in faith. Take the action your belief is spurring you to take. Clicking your heels is a choice. It is always our choice to use the amazing, loving, unlimited power we have been given. Choice — that free will thing humans have. We can decide at any time that our journey no longer has to be challenging, difficult, and daunting. At any point, we can recognize our true power within, believe in ourselves, and reclaim the good that is rightfully ours. Some questions to consider:

What if struggle isn't necessary,
and it is easier than you think?
What if you already have everything you need within you?
What if all things really are possible?

Why It's Okay to Hope

OBSERVING THOUGHTS AND BELIEFS

"And now these three remain: faith, hope, and love.
But the greatest of these is love." (1 Cor. 13:13)

Faith, hope, and love: all lovely "God words" found in the above, oft quoted scripture that deserve our consideration. Of the three words, hope is the one with which I have always had the most trouble. It never seemed to fit with the other powerfully significant, foundational words — love and faith.

We know from this Bible verse and the lines that precede it that the greatest of these is love — the most powerful force in the universe, equivalent with the omnipresent, omnipotent God-Source. We can wrap our heads around the word love. It makes sense to us on a sacred, spiritual level. Patient and kind, love is a Divine Principle, eternal and unfailing.

Faith is the foundation of our belief, the established attitude and manner in which we apply spiritual law. As students of New Thought, we know it is also our deep-seated belief in our well-being and our expectancy of good. The word faith can stand alone on its own merits. We can understand it.

But do we understand hope? For years, the word hope annoyed me because it felt half-way. Hope felt like saying: "I really want something to happen, but I am also acknowledging it might not happen." Hope seemed wishy-washy. Decidedly unfaithful. Hope has always felt to me like dreamily wishing on a star from a place of our lack, loneliness, and longing — like the sad sacks who believe the old-white-haired-man-in-the-sky-God is a completely separate power outside of themselves, who may or may not be interested in responding to their wants and desires. Yuck. Not for me, no thanks! I don't want to hope. I prefer to know.

Eventually, I discovered that I was misinterpreting the word hope and using it incorrectly. Hope is both a verb and a noun. When used as a verb, it means exactly what I described: "to want something to happen or be the case." Perhaps that is not the way the word is intended in the scripture. When used as a noun, hope actually means: "a feeling of expectation for a certain thing to happen, a feeling of trust." This explanation jives completely with the other words and makes it quite a powerful concept!

Hope, it turns out, is not about wishful thinking at all. It is about expectation, assurance, and trust. Now, I define having hope as: having certainty in the positive outcome I wish to experience while waiting patiently for said outcome to manifest into form. Sometimes it feels like we know the story of God bringing and being the light in our lives so well, that we forget we cannot truly experience light without a little darkness. Even in our darkest times, it behooves us to always trust the light. We do this by having hope. We must fully anticipate positive things and keep an expectancy of good. It isn't just a biblical virtue; it is a practical spiritual strategy to apply to our lives.

Hope is really about using our imagination in a consistently positive way, so much so that we begin to have faith and complete trust in what we are creating in our minds. Here is an easy way to remember the true meaning:

Have
Only
Positive
Expectations

Signs of Life

UNDERSTANDING THE CONTINUITY OF LIFE

Most, if not all, faith traditions have at their core a genuine belief in the immortality of the individual soul. So many religions and spiritual philosophies teach that life is eternal, and this, of course, is comforting to us, both with regard to our own mortality and when we are faced with losing our loved ones. It also just makes sense — that whatever the God of your understanding is, whatever God you pray to and believe in, would not go to the trouble of having created you only to have your life permanently end at the moment of your death. A universal theory says that we are here on the planet in physical form as spiritual beings having a human experience — here to learn and grow as eternal souls before we return to our true existence when we "die" — transitioning to some version of an afterlife, or rather, moving on to a continuation of life.

We have all heard the saying that the veil is thin (usually around Halloween, the Day of the Dead, All Saints' Day, or All Souls' Day). The phrase refers to the idea of an invisible veil separating those of us who are alive in physical bodies here on earth, from spirit guides, angels, our relatives who have left this plane, and perhaps even Spirit itself — God, Source — on the "other" invisible side. Just as there can be no duality, no sense of evil or personified devil that opposes the goodness and wholeness of God, I believe there is no "other" side. Believing that there is only one Life, one Power, one Presence, means that there cannot be any real separation between this life and the next, between this plane and another, between our life here on earth and our life with the God-Source. Any sense of separation between these things is simply a result of our lack of understanding. Maybe the veil isn't necessarily thin after all. Maybe the veil doesn't even exist!

My daughters and I were very close with my mother when she made her transition at 80 years old in 2021. We were all understandably devastated. Having studied various religions, New Thought philosophies, the afterlife, mediumship, continuity of consciousness, and Spiritualism, I shared my unique perspective with them as we all grieved. (Spiritualists believe in the continuous existence of the human soul, among other things, and often include demonstrations of evidential mediumship as part of their religious services.) My message to my girls was this: life never ends, and love never dies. Grandma was still here.

My advice to them was to remember that their relationship with their grandmother would not end just because grandma made her transition. It would simply change. We talked about signs and symbols, dreams and intuition. We discussed the importance of talking to grandma in spirit, knowing and trusting that she would hear. Just because we could not see her in person, didn't mean she wasn't still present.

A few days later, one of my daughters decided to ask her grandmother for an irrefutable sign that she was okay and still with us. She asked her grandmother to show her something random — a green lollipop. She chose it because it was simple, specific, deliberately insignificant, and not something she would normally come across in her daily life. She shared her sign request with the whole family. Several days went by.

The whole family flew to New York for the funeral, where my

mother was to be buried. It was emotional and sad, as expected, but also a little stressful and difficult. We didn't know our way around the area at all. Immediately following the service, my husband really wanted some coffee. We had rushed to the funeral home early that morning and did not have time to search for a coffee shop. We googled the nearest Starbucks™ on the way out of the cemetery. Our GPS sent us to a grocery store. That wasn't going to work. We googled the next Starbucks™ and kept driving. We arrived, got out of our cars, and as we walked in, we noticed the sign for the store next door, which was called LOLLIPOPS Children's Shop. The sign was a bright florescent green.

We were stunned and so happy, we cried! I share this story as a reminder that our loved ones in spirit are always nearby. They are but a breath away. There is no death; our loved ones still live. "Our God is not the God of the dead, but of the living, for to him all are alive" (Luke 20:38). Losing loved ones is extremely painful, but faith and belief in everlasting immortality is key to lessening the pain of the situation. When we incorporate the understanding that our loved ones still live after "death," it reveals our good in the form of peace, comfort, and the eventual return of joy. Thoughts about, memories of, and signs from our loved ones in spirit are all wonderful demonstrations of the goodness of God. Pray for them, think about them, remember them, and ask for signs from them. Make it part of the good you claim for yourself.

> *The more you believe in eternal life,*
> *the more signs of eternal life you see.*

Forgiveness: Freedom From Discord

THE POWER OF FORGIVENESS

F ounder of what we know today as the Centers for Spiritual Living religious organization, Ernest Holmes, taught spiritual practices that help and encourage people to live their best lives, experiencing fully all the good that is available to them. In his famous Declaration of Principles, published in *Science of Mind Magazine* in 1927, he wrote, "We believe the ultimate goal of life to be a complete emancipation from all discord of every nature, and that this goal is sure to be attained by all."[1] _Complete_ freedom from _all_ discord of _every_ nature? Those are some seriously absolute words and a big, lofty declaration!

What is the discord from which humans want to be freed in order to experience their good? I call the discord our *knots*. It is our disharmony, disunity, troubled relationships, lack, illness, and disease, etc. that we experience. Many spiritual practices help free us from discord, and one of the biggest is forgiveness. In fact, forgiveness may just be the answer to everything. For so many, the root cause of our discord involves holding on to a past moment and not realizing it. Much psychological study has revealed that humans have a natural inclination to not only hold on to painful experience, but to let it fester.

A great Buddhist Zen lesson illustrates this. Two monks are traveling together. They have taken vows never to touch a woman. They come upon a river with a strong current, and just as they are about to cross, they notice a beautiful young woman trying to cross. She asks them to help her. They look at each other for a second, and then the older monk picks up the woman and carefully carries her across the river. He puts her down on the other side, and she goes on her way. The younger monk cannot believe this.

The two monks continue on their journey in silence. Hours and hours go by in silence. Finally, out of the blue, the younger man says angrily, "How could you carry that woman? We are not permitted to touch women!" The old monk just stares at him and calmly replies, "I did carry her, but I put her down back by the river hours ago. Why are you still carrying her?"

So often we carry not only the hurts others do to us, but the hurts that we do to others, and the hurts that others do that might not have anything to do with us! And carrying all these hurts... hurt us. Holding on to a past moment longer than necessary causes us to harbor negative feelings and repressed emotions like anger, anxiety, fear, etc. Clinging to resentment and unresolved conflict can negatively impact our physical health. Everything from blood pressure and heart rate to the body's immune response and the occurrence of cancer has been linked to repressed emotions and a lack of forgiveness. It is imperative for our own peace and well-being that we release the past and forgive everyone. Forgiveness frees us from our burdens. Forgiveness frees us to reclaim, reveal, and recognize the good that is all around us.

So how do we do forgive? It is not a matter of flipping a switch. Forgiveness is an active process that can involve so many things, such as talking, journaling, praying, reflecting, releasing, meditating, etc. I have personally had great success with writing down what needs forgiving, sometimes in a small list format and sometimes in a lengthy letter or essay, then burning it in a fire pit in my back yard.

Only you know the process that will best help you. There is no right or wrong way to forgive. The two most important questions to ask yourself are: Whom do I need to forgive? What steps can I take to work through my feelings? When we do the work of forgiveness — and let's not kid ourselves, it is work — when we do this individually for ourselves, it ends up impacting everything around us because we are all cosmically connected in the One Mind of Spirit. When we each resolve to do this inner work, we lift the collective consciousness of our spiritual family, our local community, our country, and the entire planet.

Forgive, let go, and be free. Let your good appear.

The 51% Rule of Faith

OBSERVING THOUGHTS AND BELIEFS

Faith, if we are doing it right, comes naturally. It is a constant, calm assurance, but faith also morphs and changes throughout our lives. To get to that natural, calm assurance takes practice, and to stay there takes a lot of effort. We have all had times where our faith is rock solid. We confidently declare things like: "I am going to get through this! I am going to affirm good things and know the truth of this situation." Then we have had other times where we abandon our faith and hit panic mode. I have had times when I forgot I even had faith, when I was sobbing on the bathroom floor, angrily shaking my fist at the sky. Or maybe that's just me...

Faith is a thing of thought, meaning it takes place in our mind. It is a way of thinking and expecting, whether we are thinking good thoughts, expecting good things, or we are thinking negative thoughts and having false beliefs, expecting bad things — two sides to the same coin. It is all faith.

I have a visual tool that I use for my faith. I imagine the scales of justice in my mind. The scales represent my thoughts and words and expectations. One side represents my faith in Goodness, my knowing, my trusting, my belief in the goodness of God, Spirit, Universe, Source, Truth, etc.

The scale on the other side represents my fears. My false beliefs. My negative thoughts. The Science of Mind® tells us that fear is the negative use of faith.[1] Being afraid of things, worrying about possible bad outcomes is using our faith in a negative way. Job demonstrated that in the Bible. He said, "the thing I fear has come upon me." (Job 3:25) In a talk that he gave in 1918, Ernest Holmes said that "you cannot say a word or think a thought that is not omnipotent. That is why you bring upon yourself the thing you fear and why you bring to yourself the thing you want."[2] Good or bad, either way, we are very powerful beings.

The idea is to tip our faith scale to the Good and leave it tipped that direction. It is a little embarrassing to admit this, but when I first began studying New Thought principles and learning about using spiritual practices to improve my faith — I used to think the only way to manifest my good and really use the law was to think positive thoughts 100% of the time. I thought I had to be consciously aware of my thoughts, my beliefs, and my affirmations at all times. But that's not the way balance scales work! It turns out I was quite mistaken to think I had to tip the scale 100% to the good, positive, life-affirming way of thinking.

I would like to introduce what I call the "51% Rule of Faith." In that same 1918 talk, Ernest Holmes suggested that when just 51% of our thinking is positive, (aligned with God) those thoughts can wipe out the other 49%.[3] His numbers intrigued me and fit perfectly with the visual tool of a balance scale. It is comforting to know that it is at the slightest tip of the scale — just 51%, that we begin to see demonstration. An academic grading scale might show a 51% score as complete failure, perhaps a result of poor effort. Thankfully, Spirit operates in a much more gracious way. Having 51% of my thoughts positively focused on health, life, and power, is certainly challenging, but it feels possible!

Let this be your reminder to give yourself some grace. If you have been working with spiritual principle and feel frustrated that you are not experiencing the good you desire in all aspects of your life, that doesn't mean you are a failure. On the contrary, it may mean you are much closer than you think to consciously tipping your thought scale in the right direction. Research suggests that an average human has an estimated 6,000 thoughts per day. By this method of belief, if just 3,001 of them are positive, powerful, and aligned with God's Truth, then a demonstration of manifest good would be imminent. If we miss the intended mark today, we get up and try again tomorrow.

What percentage of your thinking do you believe is positive?
What can you do to tip your scale in the right direction?

A Chakra Balancing Guided Meditation

MEDITATION

M any ancient and contemporary spiritual philosophies believe that the human body is an energetic system made up of seven main chakras. Situated along the spine, these subtle energy wheels are associated with and can potentially influence the connection between the organs in our body and our mind, depending on whether they are open and balanced or blocked and unbalanced. It has been suggested that open, balanced chakras can promote spiritual, physical, and mental well-being. What follows is a guided meditation intended to help you imagine your way to open and balanced chakras using imagery, color, and affirmations.

Take a few deep breaths and relax. Sit in a comfortable position in a chair or cross legged on the floor. Take a moment to become consciously aware of your posture and your spine. Roll your shoulders back and away from your ears. Sit tall and straighten yourself. Obviously if you are reading this, you can't close your eyes, but soften your gaze so there is no tension around your eyes. Relax your arms at your side or in your lap. Notice your breath going in and out. See if you can slow the pace of your breathing down a bit. Imagine that floating just above your head is a glowing white light.

Take a deep breath in as you visualize this. On your exhale, allow this light to slowly move down the length of your spine. When it reaches the bottom of your spine, imagine that it continues past your spine, along an imaginary, strong, flexible cord. Let the light continue traveling down, past the chair or seat you are sitting on, past the floor, into the ground, deep into the center of the earth — straight to the core. This cord represents how connected you are, how centered and solidly supported you are by Life.

Follow the white light back up the cord, up the path of this imaginary part of your spine, back up from the earth, up through the floor, to the seat you're sitting on, and settle into the area where your Root Chakra is, at the base of your spine, right where your sit bones are. This chakra is associated with your sense of security, safety, and stability, where you know and trust that your basic physical needs are met. Imagine this white light changes to a floating ball of deep red energy. You are grounded and supported. Say to yourself, or say out loud if you wish:

I am safe.

Let the light fade from red back to white again. Move your attention up your spine to a few inches below your belly button, where your Sacral Chakra is. This is where your sensuality is, where new ideas are birthed, and your creativity lies. It is associated with your emotions, sexuality, and passion. Let the white light change to a bright orange color in this area. Imagine it spiraling beautifully. Say out loud or silently to yourself:

I am creative.

Allow the light to fade back to white, and move your attention up to your Solar Plexus Chakra, to the area just below your rib cage. This chakra is your source of power and confidence — your independence, self-esteem, and purpose. It is where your sense of willpower and motivation are. Imagine the white light beaming now as a bright ball of yellow energy, bright like the sun, radiating and spinning at just the right pace for you. Say to yourself or say out loud:

I am powerful.

As the light fades back to white, allow it to move now to your Heart Chakra at the heart center of your body. It is of course associated with love and how open you are to love, but also with our unity, balance, and compassion. Let the white color change to a vibrant green, filling your chest and radiating outward. Let this green energy represent all the Love of the Universe, the Love from which you were created, the love you receive, and the love you give to others. Say out loud or to yourself:

I am loved.

Take an extra moment to truly accept this love for yourself, before letting the green color fade back to white. Now, move the white light up to your Throat Chakra focusing on the area of your throat, neck, mouth, and jaw. This chakra is associated with your communication, your ability to listen to others, your creative expression, your voice. Let the light become a beautiful, light blue — like a bright sky, a crystal-clear blue, spinning and spiraling. Know that it is safe to express yourself openly and authentically. Say now:

I am expressive.

As the ball of energy fades back to white, move it with your attention up to your Third Eye Chakra to the area in the center of your forehead, between and slightly above your eyes. Let the color change to a deep, dark indigo blue. This chakra is associated with your intuition, your imagination, your insight, and awareness — seeing beyond your material self to your highest self. Take a moment to embrace the clarity and wisdom found here. It is always available for you to access. Declare out loud or to yourself:

I am intuitive.

Allow the light to fade to white as it moves now to your Crown Chakra at the top of your head. This chakra is associated with transcendence, meditation, ecstasy, and the recognition that you are limitless. Expand your consciousness and see if you can feel this chakra opening, spinning in perfect harmony. Imagine the light is now a deep violet purple color. This is where you sense your connection to the universe, the cosmos, and universal knowledge. Say out loud or to yourself:

I am divine.

Now, as the light fades back to white, imagine that cord, as you imagined before, continuing and extending farther up, beyond your crown chakra, where there is only pure consciousness. Imagine for just a moment you are completely untethered from this body. See if you can sense just a glimpse of how mystical you are, existing only as Source energy. This is your true self. Breathe this in! Let this fill you, empower you, inspire you.

And as you exhale, release the white light completely, coming back down to your body. Open your eyes, feeling completely balanced and aligned.

In this very moment of balanced alignment, recognize the truth available to you as your health, wholeness, and well-being.

The Light of the World

UNITY WITH THE DIVINE

Each year, I look forward to experiencing the winter solstice, which usually falls on December 21st. I may be alone in this, but I love that there is one 24-hour period where we experience the most darkness of the whole year and the least amount of light. It feels like the shortest day of the year and a day that will go by quickly because there is not much daylight. In most of the United States, people may not notice the darkness of the solstice. That is because most of America experiences 8-9 hours of daylight. It is manageable. But, in other places in the northern hemisphere, it is a very noticeable thing. For instance, in Fairbanks Alaska, they only get 3 hours and 41 minutes of daylight on their winter solstice. That makes for a very short day. Bodo, Norway, (with a population of 52,000 people in 2020) only gets about 48 minutes of daylight on the Solstice. That is it.

We know that reaching the Solstice on the calendar is like reaching that special mark, that once you hit it, it means the next day there will be just a little bit more light. And a little bit more the day after that. And a little bit more, and on, and on, more light in our world. At least that is how it will feel. People who live in darkness are really going to appreciate the solstice. It is something to celebrate because that day is a promise of the light to come. They know when they wake up the next day, there will be a little bit more light than the day before. It is guaranteed. There is no question about whether they believe that the days following the solstice will have more light. It is a planetary, natural, scientific truth that can be calculated.

The solstice is not just hopeful, it is certain. That is why it is fascinating to me that so many faith traditions and religions have holidays surrounding this scientific event that is associated with the sun having victory over darkness and this bold assurance and expectation of light coming into the world. We can trust in our faith with that level of certainty, whatever our religion or faith tradition is.

Arguably the biggest holiday around the winter solstice is Christmas, which celebrates the birth of Christ, the birth of the great example and master teacher, Jesus. The light of the world coming to earth; a promise from God. The promise is that no matter how full of darkness our life is, no matter how much we think we are separate from God, no matter how much we are living in the darkness of not understanding spiritual principle, the truth is — the light is coming. The light is there. Darkness does not prevail.

I have been on a continuous spiritual journey for many years, from various denominations of Christianity, to interfaith studies, to numerous New Thought teachings, to Spiritualism, and I have been asked if Christianity and the story of Jesus Christ still resonates with me. It absolutely does. This idea of the light of the world, this birth and incarnation, is personal to me because it is about my birth and my incarnation — my opportunity to express my individual divinity. It is personal to you for the same reason. It is personal to every one of us. God-made-flesh.

Ernest Holmes wrote in The Science of Mind®: "There can and does descend into our minds a Divinity, a Unity, the Spirit of God, the direct incarnation of the Original Thing, in us — the mystical presentation of Christ."[1] THIS is why it resonates and relates. The

Christian birth story is our story. The Divine Incarnation is inherent in our nature. The Christ light is our essence. The Spirit of God shines within each of us.

Affirm, trust, and remember that within you,
all is calm, all is bright.

The Spiritual Practice of Quitting

RELEASING WHAT NO LONGER SERVES

Most of us would agree that quitting things is frowned upon in our culture. Society as a whole generally likes winners, achievers, and successful people. Non-quitters. When we get wind of someone about to give up and quit something, we break out our pom-poms and try to cheer them into persevering. We say things like: "Never stop trying! Don't give up! Keep going! Winners never quit and quitters never win!"

To this, I say softly, but emphatically: "Shh..."

You see, I have a confession to make. Once, after much prayer, meditation, contemplation, and spiritual mind treatment, I went on a quitting spree. It was a long time coming, and afterwards, I had never felt better. I view the entire thing now as a welcomed, wonderful shift in consciousness that helped me claim and reveal my good. Quitting as a healing spiritual practice. Who knew?

Here is a list of some things I quit:

- I quit my podcast.
- I quit running my own side business.
- I quit my fairly lucrative monthly guest speaking gig.

- I quit spiritual practitioner training (that one was big.)
- I quit a long-term personal relationship (that one was even bigger.)

Why? Why did I decide to set boundaries and abandon all these things in the span of a few months? What is the larger spiritual perspective here? It began when I started paying attention to my emotions. I began tuning in to my vibration and the vibrations of the people around me and the conditions of my life. I started asking myself things like:

- "Is this work/job/relationship/program raising my consciousness or lowering it?"
- "Even though I might love doing this thing, is it energizing me or draining me?"
- "Is this situation really serving my highest good if I am experiencing pain and frustration?"
- "How would I feel if I released this situation, walked away, and quit?"

My answers were startling. I was still very unsure about becoming a quitter. So, I did what a lot of spiritual people do. I looked for God in it all. I believe that God is all there is, so, if that is true, then everything is spiritual. There must be "spiritual stuff" somewhere in all the conditions of my life — even when it feels like things aren't working right — God is in there somewhere, speaking to me. It turns out God was saying a lot.

Sometimes, when we are feeling miserable, it just means we are having a bad day. But sometimes, when it is an on-going, long-term feeling of misery, and dread, it means the Universe is telling us something is not right. It is up to us to listen. We are not supposed to be miserable. Things are not supposed to feel "wrong" in our gut. It does not mean something is wrong with us. It can simply mean we have chosen some wrong things. It does not make the things wrong or us wrong. This is not about judgement and labeling things. It just means we have the chance to make different choices.

In every moment, we are at choice. The One Infinite Power of God has so many forms that are constantly changing as the wisdom behind them changes. My quitting spree taught me that I am always at choice, fully supported and wholly loved in whatever it is I choose to experience. I have free will. I can choose to believe life is awful and my experience is miserable, or I can choose to believe life is supportive and my experience is full of the goodness of God.

Quitting is not failure, and I wish the world would stop framing it that way. It is a decision — sometimes a scary decision! Choosing to view these decisions through the lens of spiritual practice got me through all these changes. For me, it was about listening, noticing, and recognizing my intuition. The question was not "How could I possibly quit all these things and disappoint all these people?" but instead became, "Why would I tolerate feeling miserable, when this is so clearly an opportunity to listen to the Spirit of God within me and grow?"

The aftermath of my quitting spree felt amazing — better than I ever expected. Quitting can be a way of releasing what no longer serves us, and that can be very freeing. My spiritual purpose has been and continues to be honed. I feel lighter, happier, and more inspired. Just in case you are feeling burdened, miserable, frustrated, or exhausted by something you might just need to quit, know that I support you in your decision. And so does the Universe.

Let the Spirit within you be your guide to setting boundaries, saying no, releasing and quitting whatever you may need for the manifestation of your highest good.

Naturally Divine

UNITY WITH THE DIVINE

W hy is it when we hear someone say, "Oh, that's just human nature..." it is never said in a positive way? You never hear it said after something positive has taken place, for instance, when someone is being compassionate or showing kindness. It is usually said after someone is being cruel or competitive, or when we see humans exhibiting mob mentality. That is when we tend to hear, "That's just human nature!"

I would argue, NO IT ISN'T! Our human nature is that we are naturally divine, full of all the goodness of Spirit. That is what we are made of; that is what is true.

My friend and mentor, Rev. Dr. Bob Deen, reminds us of this frequently in his talks. He says, "Such is the nature of life, and the nature of Spirit, that all it asks and all it wants is the opportunity to show up. You are that opportunity. And so am I. And so it is." The congregation nods in agreement every time he says it. Yes, we are expressions of the Divine. That is our nature. We are the opportunity to show up as Spirit.

But what does that really mean?

I had a ridiculous thought. Imagine we have all been invited to the costume party of LIFE, and we are all showing up in our various costumes, just like at Halloween.

"I'm showing up as a vampire!"
"I'm coming as a witch!"
"I'm going to show up as... Spirit?"

WHAT? What would you even wear if you were going to show up as Spirit? You wouldn't have to wear anything special at all. You could come as you are because you are an expression of Spirit, naturally, simply because you exist. You are naturally divine.

Carrying this metaphor a bit further, how would people know who you are at this costume party of life? If you aren't dressed in any outwardly visible costume, people would have to recognize you by your behavior and your nature. That can be challenging. How do we know how to behave in ways that express our true divine nature?

We don't — unless we know what Divine nature is.

When I was in elementary school, my class had a party with treats and games. One of the games we played went like this: The teacher would tape a piece of paper on your back with a character written on it. You didn't get to see what the paper said. The class would give you clues about who your character was to get you to guess who you were.

I remember loving this game. I was a smart kid, and I just knew I was going to know exactly who I was when my turn came. The teacher put a paper on my back, and the class began giving me clues. I was ready! I was listening intently, and then I got very upset. I had no idea what they were talking about. I didn't know who the character was they were describing! I was frustrated, and so were my classmates! Finally, the class gave up and the teacher took the paper off my back and handed it to me. My turn was over. To this day, I will never forget what it said. It said: FLASH GORDON.

I'm sure I wanted to scream out: "Who the heck is FLASH GORDON?" You see, I had never heard of Flash Gordon. I had never read a comic book in my life, and I had never seen the popular movie that had apparently come out about the character Flash Gordon. I remember wanting to cry, and I distinctly remember wanting another turn. It wasn't fair! How could I possibly know who I was if I had never even heard of the person I was supposed to be? I had never been exposed to comic books. I had never seen the Flash Gordon movie. So, I'll say it again... *how could I possibly know the truth of who I was, if I didn't even know anything about that character or that person?*

Similarly, we cannot express our divine nature if we do not spend a little time learning about this nature. We have to know what God's nature is if we are going to fully express it. What is Divine Nature?

One of the main principles and foundations of Divine Science is the idea that because of our oneness with God, we naturally inherit the attributes and inherencies of God. As stated previously, Divine Science defines these inherencies — these fixed characteristics of God as: wisdom, love, knowledge, understanding, power, life, and joy. They list other attributes of the Divine, such as peace, health, wholeness, harmony, abundance. They call them inherencies. As you know, I like to call them "God-words."

A question to consider is, what do these words mean to us in our lives? How are we naturally expressing these things? Wisdom, love, knowledge, understanding, power, life, joy, peace, health, wholeness, harmony, abundance. These attributes and qualities are our divine nature; they are the truth of our being.

One of the reasons we want to pay attention to these "God words" and study them, meditate on them, is so we can recognize them not only in ourselves, but in others. It can be challenging to see these traits in ourselves, and it can be really challenging to see them in others.

I experienced this recently while on vacation. Traveling in airports, standing in lines at security, and getting on and off airplanes is a great opportunity to be aware of your divine nature and try to see this divine nature in others! After foolishly booking an early flight, my husband and I found ourselves in a long, winding airport security line at 4 o'clock in the morning. We kept passing this one family as the line moved. It was a mom, a dad, and two young boys.

We noticed immediately that the parents were whiners. The father was complaining that he did not get enough sleep. The hotel they had stayed at was dusty, and he was up all night coughing. A few minutes later we crossed their path again, and the mother was complaining that the line was too long, and the airport should really open up a second TSA checkpoint. The third time we passed them, one of the little boys was whining and said to his dad, "Why do we have to stay in this line?" And the father said to him, "Stop whining, nobody wants to hear your whining!" The irony amused us.

Some of our human nature we learn from our parents and our childhood experiences. Those boys may grow up to have whining, negative, complaining natures, like their parents because that is what was being modeled for them. How we are raised influences our personality, our temperament, and our nature. When we are adult spiritual seekers, no matter what we think our human nature is, we always have the opportunity to become self-aware and recognize our true nature, our true Divine nature. It takes conscious effort to bring this into our awareness.

Ernest Holmes reminds us of our truth in The Science of Mind® when he writes, "There is that within us which partakes of the nature of the Divine Being, and since it partakes of the nature of the Divine Being, we are Divine."[1] That is a big statement that makes me want to sit up a little straighter and walk a little taller. It makes me believe I have a responsibility to understand my divine nature and step into this truth of who I really am.

In a way, the royal family in England illustrates this. In June of 2022, three months before she died, Queen Elizabeth celebrated being on the throne for 70 years. The country held the Platinum Jubilee for her. There were performances and parades, and she sat with the royal family on the balcony to watch the festivities. The real star of the show though, was the Queen's four-year-old great grandson, Prince Louie.

The son of Prince William and Kate Middleton, Prince Louie was acting up during the Jubilee, and videos of his antics went viral. He was fussing, making faces, talking back to his mom, and generally misbehaving. While we couldn't hear what he and his mother were saying in any of the videos, one news agency hired lip readers to see if they could see what was being said. The lip readers believed Kate Middleton was telling Louie, "Stop it. Watch the parade," and he was saying, "I don't want to!" To which she replied, "You have to!"

One could certainly imagine the deeper meaning she was conveying to him, the deeper meaning that is no doubt taught to all the royals when they are children: "You know who you are. Be aware of your lineage. You are royalty. Choose to behave accordingly!"

Setting aside the "royal bloodline" illustration, let us take a moment to consider that we can all trace our lineage directly to Spirit, our Source. Keeping our true Divine nature in our conscious awareness inspires us to accept our role as expressions of God, expressions of Spirit. We could consider this our job, our responsibility, and our duty, but I like to think of it more as our choice, an amazing opportunity, and our great honor. We were born to recognize, understand, express, and radiate this Divine nature.

Consider this an opportunity to check in with your divine self. The call to action is to be sure that you are making every effort to fulfill your divine potential. Be consciously aware of your divine nature.

How are you going to show up as Spirit today?
Wisdom
Love
Knowledge
Understanding
Power
Life
Joy
Peace
Health
Wholeness
Harmony
Abundance

"Rejoice Always" (1 Thess. 5:16)

SEEKING JOY

J oy is a state of mind and being. Yet, sometimes, we are not feeling it. It takes some profound faith to realize that joy is not based on our life conditions, but on the constant omnipresence of God within. Joy is a human emotion, and different emotions have different vibrational frequencies. There is truth to the idea that the better we feel (meaning, the better emotions we are feeling) the more aligned we are with our God Source.

Esther and Jerry Hicks created an emotional guidance scale in their book, Ask and It Is Given. The lowest emotions on their scale are fear, grief, despair. We can go all the way up this list of 22 different emotions to the higher ones, like love, appreciation, empowerment. The highest emotion on the scale, the one that they believe most aligns us with God, is JOY.[1]

Their point is that it sometimes takes conscious effort to raise our vibration to the level of joy. So, by seeking out things that bring us joy, things that make us smile and laugh, that make us happy — doing this is actually making an effort to be closer to God.

Children do this naturally. They love to laugh and have fun. I can't help but think of the scriptures that reference Jesus wanting the children near him. They brought him joy because they instinctively understood the concept! A joyful heart and spirit are important to God.

Children bring us joy, too. That is why churches put children in their Christmas pageants. Nobody would want to sit through a Christmas play cast with adults. I have seen and directed enough Christmas pageants to know that the best part is when something goes a little wrong or really wrong and things get derailed, and the congregation ends up giggling at the children up there on the stage, just having a good time. My favorite example of this happened several years ago, when a home video of First Baptist Church of White Pine's nativity scene went viral.

For reasons I will never understand, this church decided to use toddlers only in their pageant. One of the sheep, who was two years old, decided during the Away in a Manger song, that she wanted to get up and play with baby Jesus — which fortunately, was a doll. So, she got up and grabbed Jesus and started dancing with this doll. She was just being joyful! The church roared with laughter. That wasn't even the best part!

The Virgin Mary, who was three years old, was not having any of this. She got up and tried to yank the baby Jesus doll out of sheep's hands. You can imagine how well that went over. A tug of war began, (can you hear Away in a Manger playing as this was happening?) and Mary ended up putting the sheep in a headlock, trying to force the baby Jesus doll back into the manger. Finally, the sheep's mom had to rush the stage and break up the fight as complete hilarity ensued.

Take your spiritual journey seriously, but not too seriously.
Living in alignment with joy as much as possible
helps to reveal our good.

The Car Honk Prayer

UNITY WITH ALL LIFE

W hen my youngest daughter graduated from high school, her older siblings, father, and grandparents lived far across the country, so there wasn't a lot of family present to celebrate her big milestone. Couple that with the Covid pandemic, more than a year of virtual online school, and hardly any social contact for her — I wanted to do something fun and special for her.

It started as a joke. Sometimes parents like to embarrass their children in a celebratory "I love my kid!" kind of way. Well, I had a big sign made for her that I put in the front yard. The sign read, "HONK for My 2021 High School Graduate!" Then I posted on our neighborhood Facebook page, asking for everyone's participation. I told my daughter (who of course thought I was ridiculous) that every honk was a cheer or a prayer for her future.

What happened next surprised me. As expected, the honks started coming, and from the very first one, something shifted. Something was awakening in me. I felt a connection with each driver going by, beeping their horn for my girl. I wondered what motivated them to hit that horn. Was it joy? Celebration? A prayer? A kind thought? Were they parents, too? Grandparents? Did they know her? Were they thinking of their own kids, grandkids, nieces, nephews?

Every time someone driving by honked their horn, I would scream across the house to her, "Did you hear that?!? That's for YOUUUU!!" She would shake her head and roll her eyes, convinced I was crazy. After a few days, something else started happening. She started looking forward to the honks, smiling and laughing when she would hear one. As her classes dwindled down and she got to sleep in most mornings, she would stumble out of her room, yawn, and ask me, "Did I get any honks yet today?"

"Yes, you did!" I'd tell her, because she had.

But what I really wanted to say was, "Yes, baby girl, the world cheers for you when you sleep. When you aren't even paying attention, strangers pray for your future. People who don't even know you are rooting for your success. Their positive energy is drawing out your highest good. The world is actually FULL of good people who support you and have good intentions for you. They are there — even when you don't hear their honks. Especially when you don't hear the honks. Trust this. Trust that the goodness of God present within you, is present within EVERYONE you meet. It's an energy you can feel — every time you choose to believe in it. You are SO LOVED, kiddo!"

Whatever the achievement or occasion, join me in lifting up all the young adults of the world transitioning on to the next big thing. In fact, let's broaden our intention and lift everyone up, young and old, whether they are going through transitions or simply managing to get through this human life! Let's cheer for each other! God, Spirit, Universe, Source supports our every desire. It is my hope that we hear each other's prayers and car honks.

Choose to believe in the unending goodness of Life!
Look around.
To whom can you give a cheer or honk of support?
Beep, beep!

Communion With The Father

COMMUNION/COMMUNING WITH GOD

When my father married my mother, he was Catholic, and she was Presbyterian. In order for them to get married in the Catholic church, she had to convert to Catholicism and agree to raise any children from the marriage as Catholic. So, my mom did that. (I think a little half-heartedly.) Soon my parents had my older sister. They raised her Catholic and took her to church. She was baptized, went to Sunday school classes, got her first communion, and was confirmed — all of it. By the time I came along 10 years later, my mom had, for lack of a better word, tapped-out of Catholicism. She was over it. Her attitude was: "See you on Christmas and Easter. I'm done."

So, my family didn't go to church as often. I had been baptized, but never took the Sunday school classes, didn't get my first communion, and was never confirmed. All this went on in upstate New York, where I grew up. Catholicism is very common up there, and it was all I knew as far any sort of spiritual life. By the time I started high school, we had moved to the middle of the Texas Bible Belt. My new friends brought their well-worn Bibles to school with them, prayed dramatically at the lunch table in the cafeteria, and invited me to their Southern Baptist, evangelical churches. I was spiritually confused, to say the least.

My dad explained, "That's because you're used to Catholic Church." So, he found us one in the next town over, and off we went. At this point, my sister had already moved out on her own, and my mother was still done with Catholicism, so it was just me and my father. During mass, when it came time for Communion, I couldn't get in line to receive it because I had never jumped through the appropriate Catholic hoops. My dad stayed in the pew with me. I didn't think much about it at the time. Years later, after attending and working for both a United Church of Christ and a Disciples of Christ church, (two churches that allow open table communion, where anyone is welcome to partake) I began to understand the importance of the communion ritual, what it represents, and the meaning we give it. I realized my father had made a sacrifice, staying with me in the pew all those Sundays, choosing not to receive communion for himself.

Fast forward about twenty years later,
and I'm at my father's funeral...

I had volunteered to give a reading at the service, so I was seated up on the altar in front of the whole church. There were two altar boys seated to my right, and a priest sat on my left. And then suddenly, communion was offered, and I panicked. I still couldn't receive communion, and I was at my own father's funeral! My gut reaction was to tearfully raise a fist to the sky at the absurdity of the moment. But then, I started laughing to myself because I realized... my dad wasn't having communion either. He was sitting this one out with me once again, only, he was having the ultimate communion. And he was probably laughing too, at how ironic the moment really was.

The ritual of communion can be an important part of one's spiritual experience and journey. Many progressive Christian churches make communion fully accessible, with what they refer to as an open-table. Even in that scenario, it is easy to get lost in the ritual itself, the pieces — the bread, the wine, the table, the words that are recited, etc., when what is more important is the relationship with God, the accessibility of that relationship.

The word communion is based on the word commune, which means: "to communicate intimately with." Intimacy is the key component there, a word not to be overlooked. I give great thanks for the access I have to God, always, in all ways, and for every opportunity I have to intimately communicate with this power found both within and all around me. It is worth reminding ourselves that the rituals and methods we use to commune with God are not as important as the relationship itself.

Remember, this book began with examples of rituals from various faith traditions that all led to the same place: God and the revelation of our Good. God is synonymous with our Good. Whatever the etymology, I believe there is a reason the two words are homomorphic, (sounding almost identical) in so many languages. God = good.

May you commune with the God of your understanding
in whatever way you desire.
As that relationship unfolds,
may more and more of your Good be revealed.

Good God Almighty

OMNIPRESENCE OF GOD

I have always loved personalized license plates. As a kid I remember thinking how interesting it was that personalized plates were even an option. It intrigued me — the idea that I could make my car say something and have it be on display for all the world to see. For many years my license plate was: INTRF8H (which read Inter-faith, surrounded by a frame that said: Prays Well With Others.) A personalized plate is a way to let my car express a bit of my personality. We are all expressions of God; my car is an expression of me.

So, because of this obsession of mine, I have always noticed and paid attention to personalized plates. When my kids were younger, it was a game we would play together, spotting a plate that said something. Some of the best ones we ever saw were: MUAHAHA. (What a jokester.) TIRED. (Not sure I'd want to affirm this for myself while driving, but to each his own.) The weirdest one we ever saw said: DIAPERS. (No idea why someone would want to put that that on their car. Did they make diapers? Did they have a lot of babies? Did they pay for the car by switching to cloth diapers? We had a lot of unanswered questions...)

Sometimes, it's challenging to read a personalized plate because the owner can't always fit everything on it. You get 7 characters, and that's it — a combination of 7 letters or numbers to say whatever it is you are trying to communicate to the world. So, sometimes there are things missing and you have to piece it together and figure out what it is trying to say.

One day, years ago, my daughters and I were walking in a parking lot, and we saw a personalized plate that said:

My oldest at the time was 15 years old, deep in the teenage years, and when she saw it, she shouted out, "Hey look, mom! That license plate says, it's all good!" You have to imagine the oblivious, drawled-out teenager tone. "It's all goo-ood!" She thought she was so smart.

We happened to be in a Center for Spiritual Living parking lot. So, I said to her, "We're in a church parking lot, how do you know it doesn't say "It's all God?" And she was blown away. Her eyes got huge, and her mouth hung open. She began noodling this possibility, and she was very confused. Which was it? What was the car owner trying to say? How were we ever going to know? She was determined to go into that church and find out whose car it was and ask them what it said! Fortunately, I stopped her before she started walking up to strangers and asking them. I told her it didn't matter. Because we were both right. This is the truth in which we live and move and have our being:

It's all Good, and it's all God.
This is what surrounds, animates, and expresses through you.
May you recognize it, realize it, and experience it.
It's all God, and it's all Good.

A Prayer for The Undoing

This book began by acknowledging that we all have knots — problems, challenges, and various negative experiences — from time to time. In acknowledging them, we also declare the truth that our knots are not real. They are removable, changeable, and undoable. By recognizing our unity with God, studying and applying the spiritual principles available to us, and using spiritual practices, we reclaim and reveal the good that is rightfully ours.

Let this serve as a reminder to us all that no matter what we may endure, the Spirit of God is always present. It is present in our knots, and it is present in the undoing. The Spirit of God is present in all of it because the Spirit of God is in all, including you and me. We can bring whatever good things we desire into our lives when we remember this.

Seek ye first the kingdom of God, and his righteousness;
and all these things shall be added unto you (Matt. 6:33).

It is my hope and expectation that the spiritual principles and practices offered in this book will serve as choices and opportunities for your knot dismantling. Remember, whatever method, practice, or ritual that frees you from heaviness and lifts your spirits is what you should do. A list in review:

Affirmations
Affirmative Prayer/Spiritual Mind Treatment
Communion/Communing with God
Gratitude
Intention Setting
Interfaith/Honoring All Paths to God
Law of Circulation
Loving Others
Loving the Self
Meditation
Observing Thoughts and Beliefs
Omnipresence of God
The Power of Forgiveness
Prosperity/Abundance as Spiritual Principle
Recognizing a Universal God
Recognizing Health and Wholeness
Releasing What No Longer Serves
Seeking Joy
Seeking Peace
Speaking Our Word
Stillness/Silence
Tuning in to Guidance
Understanding the Continuity of Life
Unity With All Life
Unity With the Divine

Lastly, I offer an affirmative prayer for us all as we do the spiritual work of undoing the knots and reclaiming our good:

There is only one Power, one Infinite Intelligence, one Divine Presence.
I call It God, and I know it as only Good.
It does not matter what I call it because this Power just IS. God is here in this moment, and in every moment.
It is omnipresent, omnipotent, omniscient — everywhere, all-powerful, all-knowing.
The one Power responsible for all life is in everything, including me.

I live and move and have my being in God, and I know that I am
one with God's qualities and traits.
Spirit expresses in me as harmony, peace, love, joy, health, wholeness, intelligence, abundance, and prosperity.
I am one with my good. I know this is true for me, and I know this is true for everyone.

Right here and now, I joyfully recognize the God-Presence in order to reveal my highest good.
I consciously allow a shift, an awakening to the spiritual truth that a power for good flows through me.
With this, I know that all is well.
Nothing can separate me from my good because nothing can separate me from God.
My good is at hand, and my supply is endless.

If I experience knots, problems, obstructions, confusion, I know they are not real.

I choose in this moment to release all false beliefs, negative thoughts, fear, and doubt. What I accept, reclaim, and receive in their place is my infinite, unlimited good.

My harmony, peace, love, joy, health, wholeness, intelligence, abundance, and prosperity.

This is what I align my consciousness with. This is what I say yes to!

This is what I fully expect. This is what I anticipate is unfolding in my experience now.

I give great thanks for this shift in consciousness and for the power of God.

I give great thanks for the creative process and for my ability to understand these principles and practices.

I am grateful for the opportunity to awaken in every moment, to circle back to the truth that a power for good flows through me!

I am so grateful that this is the way life works.

There is nothing left to do but release this prayer into the action of the law, anticipating its fulfillment, knowing it is done.

With great gratitude and reverence, I let go.

And So It Is. Amen.

Recommended Reading

Butterworth, Eric. *Discover the Power Within You*. Harper Collins, 1968.

—-. *The Creative Life*. Penguin, 2001.

Dyer, Wayne. *Being in Balance*. Hay House, 2006.

—-. *Your Sacred Self*. HarperCollins, 2001.

Emoto, Masaru. *The Hidden Messages In Water*. Beyond Words Publishing, 2004.

Fox, Emmet. *The Sermon on the Mount*. HarperCollins, 1989. Hanh, Thich Nhat. *Peace Is Every Step*. Bantam Books, 1992. Hawkins, David. *Power vs. Force*. Hay House, 2013.

Hay, Louise. *You Can Heal Your Life*. Hay House, 1984.

Hicks, Esther and Jerry. *Ask and It Is Given*. Hay House, 2004. Holmes, Ernest. *The Science of Mind®*. Penguin, 1938.

—-. *Creative Ideas*. Science of Mind Publishing, 2004.

—-. *Love & Law*. Penguin, 2001.

Holmes, Fenwicke. *How to Develop the Faith That Heals*. Robert M McBride & Company, 1921.

Tolle, Eckhart. *A New Earth*. Penguin, 2006.

Walsch, Neale Donald. *God's Message to the World*. Rainbow Ridge Books, 2014.

Acknowledgments

Thank you to my husband, Gary. I am grateful for your love, support, and our shared interest in all things spiritual. We are unlimited, and we know it.

I have deep love and gratitude for my daughters, who practice all this stuff without calling it anything. A special thanks to my bonus children for tolerating and sometimes even embracing the woo-woo stuff I offer. I declare good and more good for all of you!

Pam Anderson Smith, my unbelievably talented editor and friend, thank you doesn't cover it. Spirit was at work guiding me to your expertise. I am forever grateful for your genuine interest and enthusiasm. You make me shine in print, instead of sounding like a folksy idiot.

Thank you to Rev. Rich Smith, for being the person who saw something in me so many years ago. You ever-so-subtly pushed me into the pulpit before I realized I was saying good things that people needed to hear.

To CSL Reno, thank you for introducing me to Ernest Holmes. Rev. Dr. Liesa Garcia, thank you for modeling expert-level public speaking skills. You are still the standard against which I measure my talks.

Rev. Dr. Robert Deen, thank you for being interested in what I have to say, for trusting me with the CSL Midtown pulpit, and for considering me a part of the hopeful future of New Thought. Your mentorship will always be a meaningful part of my journey.

Rev. Dr. Craig M. Harris, thank you for sharing Divine Science with me in such a heartfelt, flexible, and inspiring way. You have made me feel welcomed and at home in the teaching.

Jane Slickman and Keith Reedy, thank you for your friendship, love, and all the deeply spiritual conversations we have had over cosmos.

Thank you, mom and dad, Carol and Raymond Wickes, for your signs, support, and love. Your physical transitions helped me grow in consciousness, teaching me that life never ends, and love is eternal. I had, and continue to have, the best parents!

Finally, I would like to thank God, Spirit, Universe — my source, partner, and greatest love. Being a minister and writing books may be my life purpose, but these words and ideas are all God's. I am so grateful.

Notes

Undoing the Knots

1. Ernest Holmes, Declaration of Principles, *The Science of Mind®*, (New York: Penguin, 1938) (front matter).

As We Believe

1. Holmes, *The Science of Mind®*, 280.
2. Fannie B. James and Malinda Cramer, *Divine Science: Its Principles and Practice*, Mansfield Centre: Martino Publishing, 2013), 61.

Using the Magic Words

1. James and Cramer, *Divine Science: Its Principles and Practice*, 41.

Have an Epiphany

1. Neale Donald Walsch, *God's Message to the World: You've Got Me All Wrong* (Faber: Rainbow Ridge Books, 2014), 14.

Expect Good Things

1. Fenwicke Holmes, *How to Develop the Faith That Heals* (New York: Robert M McBride & Company, 1921), 55.
2. Holmes, *The Science of Mind®*, 184

We Are One

1. Holmes, *The Science of Mind®*, 493.

Mirror, Mirror, Spiritual Practice

1. Louise Hay, *You Can Heal Your Life* (Carlsbad: Hay House, 1984), 19-20.

A Tapestry on Display

1. Holmes, Declaration of Principles, *The Science of Mind*®, (front matter).
2. Ernest Holmes, Creative Ideas (Burbank: Science of Mind Publishing, 1973), 48.

Water You Saying?

1. Masaru Emoto, *The Hidden Messages In Water*, (New York: Beyond Words Publishing, 2004), xxv.
2. Holmes, *The Science of Mind*®, 179.

We, The Chosen

1. Gailmarie Pahmeier, *The House on Breakaheart Road* (Reno: University of Nevada Press, 1998), 41.

Freedom: Who Do We Think We Are?

1. Holmes, *The Science of Mind*®, 481.

Forgiveness: Freedom From Discord

1. Holmes, Declaration of Principles, *The Science of Mind*®, (front matter).

The 51% Rule of Faith

1. Holmes, *The Science of Mind*®, 156.
2. Ernest Holmes, *Love & Law: The Unpublished Teachings* (New York: Penguin, 2001), 80.
3. Holmes, *Love & Law*, 80.

The Light of the World

1. Holmes, *The Science of Mind®*, 341.

Naturally Divine

1. Holmes, *The Science of Mind®*, 34.

"Rejoice Always" (1 Thess. 5:16)

1. Esther Hicks and Jerry Hicks, Ask and It Is Given (Carlsbad: Hay House, 2004), 114.

About the Author

Cynthia Paulsen is a New Thought Minister, licensed Divine Science Practitioner, motivational speaker, and author. Her sermons and workshops inspire spiritual growth and personal transformation. She holds an MA in Holistic Theology and has spent years studying The Science of Mind®, affirmative prayer, metaphysics, and spiritual healing.